# TRICIA GUILD'S
# PAINTED
# COUNTRY

PHOTOGRAPHS BY GILLES DE CHABANEIX

TEXT BY NONIE NIESEWAND

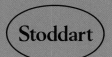

*per Riccardo*

AUTHOR'S ACKNOWLEDGMENTS
I would like to thank the following people who have all contributed to PAINTED
COUNTRY: my husband Richard Polo, who is constantly encouraging and support-
ive, and my daughter Lisa. My thanks also to Sheila and David Rainer and Ilaria
and Giorgio Miani, who kindly allowed us to photograph their houses; Adriano
Magistretti and Tom Corey, for initiating our love of Tuscany; Francesco Miani for
helping to rebuild the house; Daniella and Silvestro Baraldo and all at Bar Centrale
for delicious food and warm friendship; Nadia Morellini, Angelo Paolino and Vittore
Cosner, whose help with our house has proved invaluable.

Artists and craftspeople who have all contributed with their work – Paul and Janet
Czainski, Liz Hodges, Lisa Vaughan, Lyn Mailraith, Ralph Levy, Richard Wormesley,
Kaffe Fassett, Angela Chidgey, Lesley Harle, Valerie Roy, Tom Corey and Bill
Jacklin.

I feel privileged to be associated with such professionals as Alison Cathie, Anne
Furniss and Meryl Lloyd, who have made the book possible; Nonie Niesewand for
her energetic and voluptuous prose; Gilles de Chabaneix, whose extraordinary spirit
and magical photography is inspirational, and Samuel Bourdin and Richard Boutin
for assisting him. Thanks to Simon Jeffreys, Virginia Bruce, Sarah Wright and all
the team at Designers Guild, for their constant support and involvement, and to Jo
Willer, whose enthusiasm and effort is apparent on every page.

Editorial  ANNE FURNISS
Design  MERYL LLOYD
Production  JULIA GOLDING

Published in 1994 by Stoddart Publishing Co. Limited
34 Lesmill Road, Toronto, Canada M3B 2T6

Published in the U.K. by Conran Octopus Limited
37 Shelton Street, London WC2H 9HN

Canadian Cataloguing in Publication Data

Guild, Tricia
    Painted country

ISBN 0-7737-2802-3

1. Decoration and ornament, Rustic.  2. Interior decoration.
3. Country homes – Italy – Tuscany.  4. Cookery.  I. Title

NK1986.R8G8 1994      747      C94-930686-X

Printed and bound by Arnoldo Mondadori Editore spa, Verona, Italy

# CONTENTS

# FOREWORD

For our family, this quiet spot on a hill has become our cherished retreat. A crumbling stone farmhouse perched in a clearing, surrounded by ancient oak trees, has provided a place where I can paint my kind of picture. Whether using coloured tints or bolts of cotton, sowing seeds or preparing food, there is a transformation from one form to another. Living within the seasons and receiving from the land involves us in a more tranquil and natural existence, balancing our city life.

The challenge of restoring an abandoned wrecked building has been at times daunting. Creating a new space whilst conserving original architecture where possible and trying to develop a rapport between ancient and modern is an awesome but exciting task. There is an ongoing possibility for using my professional knowledge of colour, textile and pattern which is vital and stimulating. Trying to develop a garden and landscape that blend as one is endlessly rewarding.

We are surrounded by extraordinarily diverse sources of inspiration: landscape, architecture, Renaissance painting, the glorious frescoes found both in tiny remote chapels and in large ornate cathedrals. Or the simple pastimes of walking in the forest collecting wild mushrooms, preserving homegrown fruits and vegetables, picking fresh salad leaves and tossing them in thick green Tuscan olive oil. These are some of the vivid impressions I hope to share. The generosity and humour of local people has added a special quality to our daily life. Always a smile, an anecdote, a strong, intelligent tradition which gradually we are better able to understand. For the help they have given us we are most grateful. I sincerely hope that these pages convey some of the spirit, enthusiasm and energy given and shared by all who have contributed in turning an idea into PAINTED COUNTRY.

Tricia Guild

# A NEW ATTITUDE

## INTERIOR DESIGN TAKES A FRESH DIRECTION

Every so often, and evolving slowly over a decade or so, there is a change of direction in interior design so pronounced that it becomes a lifestyle. This is one of those times. As the eighties recede, a fresh approach can be detected, summing up the new mood of the nineties. Modern decorating can be described as a state of mind, a cherishing of place and time and a return to simplicity.

Tricia Guild's decoration of her home in Tuscany is a blueprint for this new look, revealing a set of maxims which can be summed up quite simply as follows — *Think Natural, Loosen Up, Pare Down, Colour In* and *Live Well.* "The mood I want to live with is joyful, unexpected, not stylised", she says. As the end of the millennium approaches, home becomes a place for self expression, for using what is around you and for enjoying the results. Taking her inspiration from nature, from the colours, textures and patterns of the surrounding landscape, she uses natural materials and vibrant colours to create rooms in which furniture is pared down to the minimum and simply set off with loose, untailored furnishings and unfussy window treatments. The result is a retreat from the pressures of the outside world, a haven of calm and tranquillity in which life can be enjoyed to the full.

In a world of shrinking resources we must adapt and think naturally, be environmentally friendly and resourceful to get the most from what is at hand. In fashion the trend is to loosen up, as clothing ties together and builds up in layers. Tricia Guild's new furnishing ideas are based on the same relaxed but pulled-together principle, making spaces inviting and comfortable. Banners of brightly patterned fabrics stretched across windows and entrances replace fussy window dressing to bring light and pattern into play. Colour sweeps back into our lives, vivid jolts of it to challenge the anonymity of white or black. Clutter is banished, but comfortable old sofas and chairs can see the light again, brightened up with a throw or a jewel-bright cushion — this is a time to re-evaluate what you own and revive it. These ideas encourage a mood of joyfulness and celebration, simplicity and unaffected charm. Easy to achieve, with a minimum of fuss and expense, they can be put into effect anywhere. All it requires is a new attitude.

# THINK NATURAL

## MAKE THE MOST OF WHAT IS TO HAND

The last decade left a legacy of wastefulness which a new generation attempts to redress. Though extravagant in its creativity and bathed in strong colour, in its content this book imparts a clear message for a world with limited resources: do nothing purely for effect, everything should have its function. *Think Natural* means choosing things that are honest and authentic, naturalness and simplicity winning over artifice. Even the simplest gestures make a difference – buying wicker or temperate zone wooden furniture in preference to rainforest hardwoods, for instance, or filling the house with homegrown produce, picked straight from the garden or bought in local markets.

In Tricia Guild's own home, walls are softly burnished with a pure plaster skim, borders are painted at skirting board and dado height to introduce changes of colour above bare stone floors, whitewashed rafters give the illusion of height, and open hearths are filled with baskets of dried lavender to scent winter fires. The windows are free of curtains and hung with boldly patterned banners of fabric that tie simply onto poles. Her designs are environmentally sound but contemporary in their restrained use of natural materials and honesty of function, while the unpretentious look still celebrates comfort.

Maize ripening on stalks against honeyed brick walls, papery skeins of garlic strung from rafters the colour of grass after the hay has been harvested, parchment and vellum set against each other – all the neutrals and naturals she uses celebrate shape and texture. Keeping to a neutral, natural palette with bleached sand and stone, wood and wool, gives one the opportunity to explore different materials which will bring texture into play. Textures give a room atmosphere – hard or soft, rough or smooth, glossy or matte – and change seasonally. The feel of cool stone slabs underfoot in summer when light muslin hangs softly from wrought iron curtain rods to filter the light, wool with damask and patterned Persian paisley throws in winter, rough sisal on the hard wintry floor.

Nature is a most rewarding source of inspiration. Absorb and learn to make the most of what is around you in the fields, woods and hills for your palette in design, for food and flowers or for table settings. Having a garden enables you to bring in its produce to preserve or dry for the winter months, but even pots or window boxes can be put to use growing herbs or salad leaves. The modern country cook eats homegrown and cooks from her region. When you are in touch with nature no season passes unnoticed: in winter you can enjoy the fruits of spring and summer labours, with logs and scented herbs for the fires and fruit and vegetables preserved or dried in the last of the summer sun.

Being resourceful and using what is already there can be as simple as roping in a courtyard branch and tying across a metre of fabric to make a shady outdoor room. A sun deck that invites nature in and entices people out can be shaded by a piece of fabric slung vertically between two poles; a pergola created naturally and instantly – with a fabric awning. Seating can be as basic but good-looking as a farmhouse chair and a stone slabbed bench with white linen cushions, lit by a lantern for al fresco meals at night. Thinking naturally can be applied to creating a terrace with sea-washed pebbles laid in a pattern on the earth to make a cobbled courtyard. So honest materials are recast in new, more imaginative roles.

Much of going green at home is based on gestures, both large and small. Use homegrown lavender to fill bags for linen closets rather than mothballs; choose water rather than oil-based paints, light your home inside and out with candles or lanterns to save electricity and simultaneously enjoy their soft light. Dispense with extravagant packaging and plastic carrier bags in favour of local baskets. When buying furniture, avoid endangered hardwood and choose sustainably-grown species.

# LOOSEN UP

## MIX AND MATCH FOR CASUAL COMFORT

Just as in fashion the tightly fitting tailored look of the last decade has given way to a looser, more casual style, furnishing becomes freer. The elaborately pelmeted, swagged and tied-back window treatments that were so fashionable give way to simpler, unlined banners of colourful fabric tied with tapes to a curtain rod or pole. Linen summer curtains get a winter plaid tied on top; yellow and emerald silk taffeta curtains are draped and swathed simply over the rod for a casual curtain heading when not drawn. Tie-backs are mere twists of the off-cuts, or pieces of fringe in a contrast colour. Today it's the mix, not the match, that makes a room work.

The new approach is to humanise, not harmonise. Co-ordinated, overdressed interiors are just made to be taken apart in the way the deconstructionists have taken apart fashion. Simple touches that will enliven a room include framing the view from a small window with a trailing vine outside, or banding its thick sill in bold colour and adding a small kerchief in lime and turquoise and lemon-striped taffeta. Upholstery, too, can be as relaxed as these bannered windows, but it's not necessary to overspend in order to make changes. Overstuffed, piped and valanced sofas and chairs can be transformed with the use of fabric. An occasional chair becomes a conversation piece with the addition of just two metres of patterned material lined with a brilliant two-colour plaid. Make an upright, uptight, moss green upholstered sofa casual and comfortable with a mango and turquoise plaid throw and a scattering of cushions in persimmon, apricot, lime and pomegranate — all the colours of a Caribbean fruit plantation. A pair of plain wicker chairs moves indoors gracefully with a slipcover; an old club chair gets a white linen throw so capacious it moulds it firmly to tuck into the arms and still falls in folds to the floor; a pole slung across an entrance with a bold strip of fabric changes a dull wall into a work of art.

Loosening up can also describe a mood, as well as influence tailoring. Learn about soft light from candles or table lamps, and watch how the light changes rooms from winter to summer, even from midday to dusk. Choose natural textures such as linen, cotton and wool, for their good feel, then add leafy natural patterns with fruit and flowers. Understand how to make spaces flow into each other with details such as a continuous painted border and make adventurous new entrances with doors and shutters in contrast colours. Frame the view with banded borders around window frames or with a simple piece of fabric cleated onto a wire. Loosening up in the garden can be achieved by seeding and growing your flower borders in pots, to move around where the mood takes you, or letting the daisies take over a lawn. String a hammock between fruit trees for a place to pause; plant sage and lemon balm, thyme and camomile between flagstones to scent the air near the kitchen door.

These fast, affordable ideas can rejuvenate your home, and while they loosen up daily life in the most agreeable way they are also testimony to functional living. Casual charm does not mean inefficiency. In the kitchen, labour-saving appliances are included, but hidden behind rustic wooden facades. Mixed, not matched, wooden units can be found in local markets; all the necessary utensils are hung from painted wooden shelves on which are stacked jars of ingredients and homemade preserves. All in view and easy to hand, this is the place where friends gather to gossip and work together, where produce is brought indoors to fill the baskets, where food is cooked and prepared. These newly-relaxed attitudes never need become sloppy thinking, if you plan your space properly, in proportion, so that one value never outweighs another; and make sure that in its simplicity and friendly appeal the object or utensil is still functional.

Loosening up means putting together the things you really like, whether or not they mix and match, and making them work together in a relaxed grouping by pulling together the colours, patterns, textures or shapes. These simple effects cost little and require no particular skill or sleight of hand to achieve, but they will provide a feeling of relaxed well-being in your home.

# PARE DOWN

## MINIMISE TO MAXIMUM EFFECT

In this contemporary view of country style, alongside the simple, natural approach is the requirement to prioritise your needs. To create fresh, modern interiors in country rooms with a minimum of architectural detail needs careful decoration and furnishing. Colour and pattern must be introduced in a pared-down, pure way and few pictures or wallhangings are allowed to interrupt the fluid lines or broad sweeps of colour on the walls, floors and ceilings. These are the largest areas of uninterrupted colour and texture and they can be treated alike, in a harmonious scheme, or differently. Then move to the doors and windows to complete the structure.

Paring down means defining the space, refining the clutter and allowing self expression with furnishing. Fewer things of better quality illustrate the pared-down approach. Resist the urge to clutter up your rooms and allow furniture to double up, inside and out, with a change of cover or the addition of a colourful cushion or throw. Ask yourself what you really need and take inspiration from the landscape, where traditionally the countryside and its inhabitants' needs were reconciled. Functional can still be beautiful, as the Shakers proved. Famous for the simplicity of their work and the plainness of their day-to-day life, they had no room for the purely aesthetic, yet their well-crafted tools and utensils have a simple beauty of their own.

Everyone's needs are different. Our enthusiasms will determine the essentials and, consequently, the focal points. What you put in will transform empty rooms into spaces full of character that meet individual demands, and that individuality brings character – and style – to a home.

The message is simple. A home needs a few basics – the sofa, the bed, the chair (easy and dining and working) and the table for eating, working and display. After that it depends how you wish to use your space. Begin with a sense of purpose, a plan. Few people start with no belongings or furniture at all, but it is important firstly to evaluate what you have before you pare down. Ask yourself how many people are likely to sit around your dining table, and this will tell you how many chairs and how much storage space for china you will need, then get the most flexibility from a number of options. Diminishing space and fuller working hours may mean that there is more need for modern desktop equipment than entertaining space, for example. But just because you work from home and have fax machines and spreadsheets, there is no reason why your workspace should not be good-looking and comfortable. Try to reconcile basic functions with comfort and the possibility for relaxation, and plan an energising colour scheme to facilitate your work. For office storage, resist buying ugly, badly-made systems that you cannot live with and keep your hardware or papers in old pieces of country furniture found in local markets.

You don't have to buy it, just rediscover it. Re-invent familiar things in a new setting. A successful furnishing scheme is one that gives you pleasure and does not pall. Often, the more elaborate it is, the more wearisome it will become. As interior decoration becomes less theatrical, less like scene painting on a grand style, pare down your special effects to idiosyncratic touches, such as a rococo lamp with low voltage light which has no need of a shade, or a window dressed simply with a flag of fabric tied onto ribbons. In understated rooms they are just as dramatic as the buttoned-up, swagged, braided, frilled and furbelowed upholstery of another age.

# COLOUR IN

## CHOOSE A PALETTE TO SUIT YOUR SURROUNDINGS

Colour is the easiest, and least costly, way to transform a room. It can make a room smaller or more spacious and, above all, create energy. Develop the colour palette that works best for you by looking about you at the landscape. The blue of the Tuscan sky, the ochre of the fertile soil, the green vineyards and grey olives, the terracotta pots and the punctuation marks of dark green that the cypresses bring to the landscape have all influenced the way in which Tricia Guild has coloured her home in Italy. The sun-ripened colours of the landscape are sparked by jolts of vivid, accent colours as seasonal as fresh spring greens, acres of golden yellow sunflowers in midsummer, poppy red and corn-stubble yellow in autumn and earthy ochre in winter.

The colour flow is uninterrupted, which makes for peaceful, meditative spaces. Like a vivid thread connecting the different levels of the house is a slate blue-green base at skirting board level, demarcated with a rose and black-and-white fine line. Above it, walls are painted in many shades of sunshine yellow, or soft terracotta, or vivid blue to enliven the space. The combination of plastered walls beneath high raftered ceilings and stone floors might have seemed cold, but is softened with layers of applied colour. Green is calming and restful, reminiscent of summer fields and fresh new growth. Blue is expansive, watered like the sea and the sky. Yellow is warming and positive like the sun, whilst red is used as an accent colour. In the sitting room, blue and white with aquamarine, turquoise and lime green make a shady retreat from the heat of summer, warmed up in winter with crimson, orange and yellow by way of different curtains and cushion covers. The monochromatic blue of the main bedroom evokes serenity, as opposed to the vibrant energy imparted by the limes, yellows, apricots and emerald of the study.

After decades of plain painted walls and solid colour carpeting, backgrounds are back, with layers of pattern on pattern, textural contrasts and brilliant colours. How the colour is applied is as important as the actual shade. In this case it is sponged on or applied in several coats and layers peeled back to reveal other colours for a broken, softened effect. The secret to distribution of colour around the home lies in how much or how little is used, and in an understanding of the effects of individual colours. The more subdued the tone, the more peaceful. The cool colours of the blue/green spectrum are ideal in the southerly, warm-toned sunlight of Tuscany. Colours in the yellow/red spectrum are known as warm colours and can make a space brighter, or, used in inverse proportions with red taking over from yellow, they can make a space feel smaller and more intimate. White is a colour, too, from the pale ivories to silvery moonlight whites. Strong light will intensify white, which is why it is so effective used as a foil to blue in the islands of the Aegean.

The perception of a room's height can be influenced by the counterplay between wall and ceiling colours: the darker the ceiling colour, the lower it appears, while dark walls with a light ceiling increase the sense of height. Colour choices can be dependent upon direct or indirect natural light, as well as the direction the light comes from. Tester cans of paint will help you to see how colours react to different lights over a twenty-four hour period. Paint and paper will take on a different colour in your own home. For example, a predominantly white colour scheme can seem creamy in a south-facing room bathed in warm sunlight but take on a bluish tinge in a north-facing room. A west-facing room takes on the warmer light of afternoon, while an east-facing one will reflect the colder light of morning.

Since the response to colour is more emotional than rational, its choice must be individual, but what is to be learnt from Tricia Guild's palette is the way in which one colour sparks off another, and just how much of the contrast or accent colour is needed. A glance out of the window assures us that nature has teamed blue with green, but it is rare to find two such strong colours in juxtaposition through the length and breadth of a house. Colouring in calls for an adroit balance between colours of equal intensity.

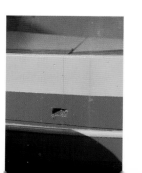

# LIVE WELL

## CREATE AN ATMOSPHERE OF TRANQUILLITY AND WELL-BEING

The most wonderful memories are of time shared, meals enjoyed, rooms with a view, joyful colours, peaceful places. Good health, relaxation, comfort, nurture, friendship and love — these are the elements of good living. Tricia Guild's attitude to making a home does not stop with the colour of the walls and the furnishings — it extends to every aspect of her life. For her, a home should be filled with flowers and scents from garden and kitchen, with music and laughter and love.

Living well can be found in simple pleasures: a profusion one autumn of damsons, or mushrooms, when blackberries are clustered on the hedgerow brambles, free for the picking; a glut in the garden resolved into full-bellied jars of preserves, tawny or crimson, amber and purple for use in the winter; the first daffodils heralding spring; a midsummer meadow filled with wild flowers. It can be about a peaceful walk with friends on a balmy evening. Country life is based upon self reliance, a quality captured here as though held in a bell jar, its essence distilled to give us fresh hope for the future.

In the country, living well can mean an abundance of fresh produce, whether homegrown or homemade. Flowers, greenery, fruit and vegetables gathered and brought into the home can be used decoratively or cooked and served on colourful, ceramic plates and bowls. A painted wooden table draped with an embroidered cotton cloth and laden with produce fills us with pleasurable anticipation just as a windowbox, or pot outside the kitchen door, can provide herbs to scent the home and flavour regional dishes. Outside, a garden can be as small as the site is level, or so large that it can be divided into separate areas by espaliered trees or clustered pots. A small backyard, a terrace, a patio or even a balcony in the inner city can be turned into an enchanting place if you scale down the ideas shown here, using bowls and pots for plants that can be moved at will. With a bit more space you can make an outdoor room. The basics are simple garden furniture and a fabric awning, with plants scrambling up wooden poles or arches to form the framework.

Living well also means blurring boundaries between inside and out, with awnings and pergolas that cool the air as it enters the house, allowing hot air which rises to flow out. A parasol becomes the centrepiece of a cluster of wicker chairs and tables. As furniture moves out, or in, so do the candlesticks and lanterns. On a summer's night, a spontaneous meal served out of doors is more fun. Masses of night-scented flowers, wild or planted, tumble from pots or buckets, modern ceramic or clear glass vases. Bring out the colour with blue-and-white speckled china bearing seasonal food, cotton napkins found in a local market, painted wicker chairs with comfortable cushions.

Indoors, fill ordinary household buckets with flowers and greenery or a simple glass vase with wild red poppies, sited where you can open your eyes in the morning to their pure colours and delicate fragrance. Pile dark green vegetables and glowing peaches into baskets to celebrate their sun-ripened plumpness.

Tricia Guild's recipes address the need to cut fats, reduce the amount of meat eaten and achieve top physical and mental well-being by eating nutritious fresh garden produce. Modern country cooks leave no source untapped in their search for the best quality, enjoying markets or farm shops which provide flavoursome, seasonal food. Food always tastes best served simply and without fuss — dappled green plates laden with spears of asparagus and slivers of local cheese announce the arrival of summer; a warm damson tart celebrates autumn's harvest; a hearty soup warms a cold winter's day. Combining the best of local ingredients into dishes which look and taste delicious gives pleasure to cook and guest alike, bringing a sense of well-being to all who eat together in friendship.

# THE PAINTED HOUSE

## TRICIA GUILD'S RESTORED FARMHOUSE IN TUSCANY

Few regions of unspoilt countryside have been painted as much as this southern slice of Tuscany, with its views of vineyards, softly rolling hills, olive groves and medieval hilltowns unchanged since the Renaissance. It is a place that positively encourages self expression. The new attitude to decoration shows in Tricia Guild's house, where she celebrates her love of colour and nature in the clean, uncluttered lines of the interior, furnishing it in a carefully studied style of relaxed informality.

The farmhouse was derelict when she discovered it, gaping holes in the masonry indicating where the windows once were and one wing tumbling down the hillside upon which it is perched. The central core (where the entrance hall is today) is the oldest part of the house, dating back to the twelfth century. Animals were penned here at night, while the inhabitants occupied the first floor, reached by an outside staircase. Before restoring the structure, Tricia Guild drew up a plan of the space, keeping the bedrooms on the first floor, in two wings linked by the original living room with its old fireplace. Adjoining each bedroom a bathroom was carved out of the space, carefully sited so that the exterior was not disfigured by a mass of pipes. A new staircase was built to link the entrance hall below to the bedrooms and the original outdoor staircase was restored to reach a little balcony opening into the first floor sitting room. Leading from the entrance hall downstairs is the sitting room and adjoining study. Where the house had fallen away, a new wing was built to house the kitchen and dining room, linked by an open hearth. Throughout the rebuilding and restoration the regional style of architecture was maintained, both in design and in the use of local materials. From outside the solid stone-walled farmhouse there is no hint of the brilliant interiors that await within.

The following pages take you on a photographic tour of the finished house, focussing on those elements that can be adopted, or adapted, to suit any location. Following this chapter and to show how easily Tricia Guild's fresh ideas will travel, there are views of three neighbouring houses in Tuscany and one house on a Greek island which present variations of this new attitude to country decorating.

To retain the original features of the vernacular building the ground floor was lowered to give the rooms more height, without losing the chestnut rafters that supported the first floor. Roof tiles and stone blocks from the ruined buildings were salvaged and used in the rebuilding. The small windows, traditionally tiny to keep out the noonday sun but keep in the heat when temperatures drop at night, were restored; fanlights were added above the original doors to let in more daylight. So, a virtue is made of necessity and the house still sits companionably beside its neighbours, as unobtrusively and harmoniously as it has done for centuries. Nevertheless the adjustments made for modern living have taken place — the kitchen is filled with modern labour-saving appliances, the study houses a fax, lighting is contemporary, the warmth from the hearth is backed up with radiators.

The vernacular style of architecture also encouraged Tricia Guild to develop a particular style of furnishing and decoration. The small windows suggested banners of fabric tied onto poles, rather than elaborate window dressing. That, in turn, led to a more relaxed style of comfortable seating, without fringes and piping. Inside Tuscan farmhouses it is traditional to paint a broad band around entrances, outlining rooms where in other houses the skirting board and cornice would delineate the space. She revived this tradition with wide borders in chalky pinks and limes, bordered in turn with fine-lined grid patterns.

Plain walls are a positive invitation to be daring. The bold background is back and a tour of this house reveals how simply these dramatic effects can be achieved. Each room has its own colour borders on the walls and there is a sequential flow in the colour scheme that leads the eye forward to the next space. In contemporary buildings where there are no mouldings or architectural details, this simple idea can make rooms interesting. Layering colours over each other and applying a final glaze, or rubbing the coats before drying with a damp sponge, will bring a softly burnished, dappled effect to paint, which is far more interesting than several coats of the same colour. In this house, Tricia Guild has overturned some conventional decorating maxims: for instance, she has used blue, commonly held to be a cold colour, to great effect in her own north-east facing bedroom where the light is soft. By combining this revised approach to decoration with vernacular traditions and a bold use of colour, she has created an interior that is in harmony with its regional roots but at the same time reveals a new attitude to contemporary living. She sought inspiration in the Giotto frescoes in the cathedral at Assissi, in the amazing black and white patterns of Siena, in the richness and quality of light in Piero della Francesca's frescoes in the tiny chapel in Monterchi, where the plain brick building gives no hint of its dazzling interior.

Within, she felt that the house needed strong lines on simple furniture. Old farmhouse chairs sit comfortably with rustic benches, early Biedermeier with mid-century modern, wire and iron with wood. Objects and spaces have value because they work not only on a functional level, but also on an emotional one. Getting the balance right in the mixture of periods and pieces is as critical as the space in between.

As important to Tricia Guild as the restoration and decoration of the building was the landscape immediately surrounding the house. Two fertile acres of rich red soil with unimpeded views across the rolling hills were staked out around existing trees. Little sitting areas, reached by paths edged with box, lavender or rosemary, are demarcated with benches and chairs, and sometimes framed with a pergola. A vegetable garden next to the kitchen is laid out in colourful squares of blue and red. The borage, thyme and sage that butterflies love clusters amidst sweet peas and the silvery foliage of artichokes and rosemary. Opposite, cherry tomatoes, strawberries and nasturtiums glow amidst the arugula and salad leaves. Paths are edged with box and banks of lavender, geranium and rosemary scent the air.

To allow more light to fall upon this impressive hallway at the core of the house, the thick stone walls into which the front door is set are painted white and the door panels are glazed, protected by shutters painted a pewtered grey-green. Rather than lose the original low-beamed ceilings of the lower level of the building, the floors were dropped at ground level, then laid with honeyed old flagstones, smoothed by the tread of centuries. Above, a few steps lead up into the guest suite whilst on the other side of the hall the main staircase leads to the upper floor. The colours of the house are gently introduced in the hall with painted borders in the vernacular Tuscan farmhouse tradition: broad swathes of slate-coloured grey-green delineate the room at skirting board height and climb up to colour the stair risers; each doorway is demarcated with a band of lime. These are the colours of the surrounding landscape: fresh spring green dampened with the grey-green of olives and the sunny yellow of the hay at harvest. A stolid wooden table painted turquoise serves as a console table.

In the original building, the only access upstairs was via a narrow flight of stone stairs outside. The new in door staircase which now links the two storeys of the house is deliberately unobtrusive. Along a ledge at the top a set of watercolours is casually propped to be seen upon ascent to the bedrooms. A sharp lime painted line joins the slate green skirting as it runs upstairs.

These bands of colour unify the house, taking the eye along a sequential path that follows the architecture, while different textures introduce new colours. The strongest colours are used on painted furniture and with fabric on upholstery and at the windows. Changes in texture which break up the application of colour are important to the scheme.

The nasturtium colours of orange, lime, yellow and fresh green applied by the ceramist Liz Hodges to her pots (left) are both in harmony with ancient Tuscan culture and yet very modern, which is why they sit so well in the modern interior of this old house.

The hall leads into the sitting room with a subsequent change of direction in the pattern of the floor tiles and the wall colour altering from whitewash to a soft terracotta. Like an original plaster skim, this chalky pink brings a glow to the vivid upholstery and wooden furniture, highlighting the myriad greens and shocking pink of a painted table against the wall. At the large squared entrance to the sitting room, banded with lemon and lime, the smooth, curvaceous lines of a Biedermeier chair at an old table piled with papers take the eye forward into the room. Sophisticated rustic is the mood. This seemingly artless style allows the unrelated collection of old and new furniture within the room to work as a group. The quirky lights on the table are typical of the contemporary approach to lighting in the house. Low voltage halogen lights in directional, angled, modern fittings are placed in considered spots such as bedside tables and worktops as task lights. For relaxation in the sitting areas and for dining, the flickering light of candles illumines without focussing on any specific object.

# SUMMER SITTING ROOM

In the sitting room, a big plaid sofa piled high with cushions becomes the most inviting place in the house. Both glamorous and comfortable, the upholstery in fresh mint and white is the perfect background for plumped-up cushions in many patterns and colours. Silk taffeta striped in lime and emerald, polka-dotted cotton and red and gold silk plaids are both seductive to the eye and to the touch. Despite the predominance of fabric, the bright colours with their white highlights make this a refreshingly cool room, shielded by thick walls and small deep-set windows from the baking heat of the Tuscan summer. The fresh greens of the upholstery move across to dress the far window, where the wooden frame is outlined in the same shade and a simple banner of fabric with an indigo border is tied to curtain rods. The scale of furnishings, large offset with small, is carefully planned so that no one size can dominate the room. The fireplace and the deep sofa, built to seat many, are cut down to size by small tables placed nearby.

# WINTER SITTING ROOM

At the end of summer a change of furnishings signals the drawing-in of the days and warms up the sitting room for comfortable evenings by the fireside. Using deeper, more sensual colours, the whole feel of the room changes.

Cushions, blanket throws and additional curtains are inspired by the cheerful crimson, orange, yellow and lime greens of autumn zinnias. Crimson and gold are the base colours of woollen plaid throws which tuck into the evergreen and white upholstered sofa, replacing the cooler blues and greens of the summer accessories. Purple and green artichokes and the damsons that drop from laden trees in late autumn inspired the deeper accent colours for plaids and fringes.

Underfoot a sea-grass mat is laid to cover the hard tiled floor. Unlined, large-scale, red-checked woollen curtains are simply tied onto the same rings over the existing summer cotton banners to hold the chill of winter nights at bay.

Thicker fabric around the extremities and warmer colours on the sofas and chairs have the effect of reducing space and re-centring the room around the blazing hearth. At the first sign of spring, all these warm covers and curtains are just folded up and stored away in cupboards with scented cotton lavender bags.

On one side the sitting room leads onto a terrace which also connects with the dining room and provides a casual and sheltered place to eat. Instead of a cloth, bold stripes on the table are freely hand-painted. Pulled up around it, an old wooden bench and rusty little metal chairs found in a local shop add to the informal setting.

Flowers are found throughout the house whatever the season. In keeping with its relaxed atmosphere the arrangements are always simple, often just one or two flowers placed amidst herbs, or leaves or grasses in a speckled or polka-dotted jug. Tricia Guild has found that growing her own flowers has added to her appreciation of their individual beauty. In a vase, the leaf size, shape and texture are as noticeable as the colour, and she contrasts the feathered bergenia leaves with the nasturtium pad, or the squat hosta with an escallonia trail. A container can be as basic as a tin bucket or as precious as a handmade ceramic piece, so long as it has personality and an interesting shape. Its origins are meaningless, hence the use of an old inkwell to support a single nasturtium.

The table setting itself becomes another means of self expression. Plates, dishes and napkins are rarely matched, but an individual assortment of hand-painted or collected items held together by sun-splashed colour and pattern. Painted squares of fabric or off-cuts from the local market appear as tablecloth and napkins, the whole scene brought to life with fresh flowers and beautiful glassware.

# THE STUDY

The full stop to the house, the last room on the lower level, is the study. Reached through the sitting room, the greens of that room are picked up and sharpened with more yellow in place of the blues. Like a finale, the design is heightened with vibrant tones of lime and mango, orange and green, while poppies and sunflowers provide the inspiration for a needlepoint chair. A change of pace introduced by the stronger colours and textures brings energy to this small, low-ceilinged room. Suddenly, lime green borders painted to dado height anchor the room, emphasized by a lemon stripe between blue bands. Stripes change to plaid as these colours are picked up and added to in curtains at the little window and door. Light floods into the room through double doors and tiny windows, all additions to a previously dark, musty stable, but so in keeping with the style of building that they could have been there for centuries. Windows and door are minimally dressed because of their size, the unlined banners glowing in the bright light.

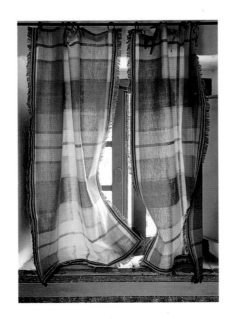 

Throughout this house, it is noticeable that wall space is mostly freed from shelves and pictures, bare but softly painted in glowing colours that demand the same emotional response as an abstract painting. Free of clutter and distractions to the eye, these walls washed in colour allow space to flow uninterrupted through room after colourful room. The choice of colours evolved over time in each given situation. This room, intimate and cosy, a retreat from the busy world, is nonetheless a workplace which has been consciously electrified by the strong sunflower colours. It is thus much more activating than the serenity of a pale blue room, for instance, or the calm workmanlike purposefulness of natural wood. Emotional satisfaction is a function of good design. Here, the texture of the roughened woods with their many-layered painted colours psychologically brings depth to the room, adding contrasts and richness. Colour brings this space to life.

As its name implies this room is for quiet study, for reading in the comfort of the cushioned sofa, for listening to music or for working. Within its four walls are all the modern communication necessities of the late twentieth-century household, but none are on show. A single table and chair, a desk tucked into the corner, are the only indications that this is a place for concentration, the rich colours an aid to focussed attention.

Co-ordinating strong colours in a scheme like this one can be a complicated affair, but close examination of Kaffe Fassett's hand-stitched chair in this setting shows how such colours not only resolve their differences in close proximity to each other, but can then be taken and distributed around a room. Royal blue, luminous lavender, deep purple, grass green and turquoise with sunny yellow are stitched together in this design of fruit and flowers. These colours, or tones of them, appear here and there around the room in a pot of sunflowers, a coloured ceramic bowl, on roughly-painted wooden surfaces and upon upholstery, cushions and throws.

As well as the colour, it is the proportions in this cosy but uncluttered room that make it work. The area of the yellow gingham sofa is lightened with white and intensified with the fresh green on the neighbouring upholstered plaid chair. A balance is achieved between the large painted wooden cupboard, the small table next to it and the little spindle-legged bench beside the sofa. The space is also modified by the light coming into the room.

The study opens out onto this terrace, perched like a treetop hideout over a precipitous drop to the valley below. The land had fallen away down the slope, so all the earth excavated when the floors were lowered on the ground floor was brought round and packed down to create the terrace. This was then clad in cement, laid with terracotta tiles and studded with pebbles. On this newly-created terra firma, pattern holds the floor with rows of tiles bordering pebbles to anchor a group of chairs and tables. To link inside with out, the vivid yellow, blue and green from the study are intensified as solid colour spray-gunned onto the wicker chairs. Softened with mango plaid throws and cushions in blue and white gingham, this grouping becomes a cheerful little meeting point for a mint julep or an iced tea. Ferns and plants in pots decorate tables in this sitting room without walls, contrasting happily with the natural abandon of hollyhocks growing on the hillside.

# THE DINING ROOM

Although the house features many eating places, both indoors and out, the dining room is always an expectant reminder of good times spent around the table, still the focal point of a rich and varied conversational life. Undoubtedly it comes into its own at night and in the winter, when the hearth that divides the room from the adjacent kitchen is ablaze and the flicker of candlelight from the orbed Italian candelabras illuminates evenings spent around the solid, turn-of-the-century table. Facing east onto the treelined hillside, this room receives less daylight than any other, so its small windows have no hangings or curtains that would cut out the light. Instead, the thick stone sills are painted golden yellow and framed with vivid blue stripes to catch and enhance any daylight filtering through. Yet more luminous colour is added below the windows with walls painted primrose yellow, edged at dado height with fine lime-green borders narrowly delineated in the same blue. At the same level, an assortment of painted chairs with rush seats makes an informal grouping around the table.

In summer, when the room is not much in use, the dining room table is dressed with a long linen runner sold by the metre for tea towels at a local haberdashery stall. It is the perfect crisp backdrop for a trio of iron candlesticks, ceramic platters and willowy branches of broom in a yellow jug. An old tongued and grooved wooden meat safe rubbed with aquamarine, indigo and green to a luminous shine houses drinks and glasses, while a campaign table stores trays ready to be loaded and carried out of doors on summer evenings. Unmatched furniture, like unmatched tableware, has so much more character than a six-piece dining suite, which would somehow be inappropriate in this raftered space. Instead, simple kitchen chairs are drawn up around the cherrywood table. By keeping the emphasis low, with brightly-coloured walls, all the furniture below the level of the painted dado rail and candelabras hung low over the table, the room gives an illusion of greater height than its low-beamed ceiling permits.

# A MODERN COUNTRY KITCHEN

Hanging in Tricia Guild's kitchen is a coloured pencil drawing entitled 'Living with Lyn' of another colourful kitchen, under which is this message: 'The kitchen, a place bursting with colour and energy — bright colour, checks, plastic table covers and tins and jars — adventure and spontaneity.' No coincidence that it should be hanging here for, apart from the plastic table covers, this kitchen conveys all of that colour, energy, spontaneity and adventure, along with a certain reassuring familiarity in the use of tiles, wood and stone. Although recently built and containing every modern convenience and labour-saving appliance hidden behind old farm gate fronts, it has the comfortable air of an old and settled place. The flagged stone floor, the rush-seated chairs, the farmhouse table adorned with its carved wooden coronet festooned with essential cook's equipment, have the friendly familiarity of an age-old work place. This arrangement is proof that expensive manufactured units do not make the kitchen more efficient, or the food any better.

The thinking cook's kitchen is planned for efficiency. A dedicated cook is at work here, experimenting with new recipes, cooking naturally with spontaneity and gusto. Shelving is strictly hands-on — there are no sliding drawers, expensive carousels or modular units. One wall houses the pantry with steel shelving. Along the other, above the gated units, the hard, practical worktop, custom-made from flecked, slate-grey local stone is ranged with jars containing cook's utensils: whisks, wooden spoons, knives and chopping boards. The deep, shaded east-facing window sills maintain oils, vinegars and eggs at a constant cool temperature. Within easy reach to the side of the cooker are shelves housing baskets of cutlery. On the walls above sink and hob every item from sieves and measuring jugs to tea towels and cooking utensils hangs from blue painted bracketed shelves. Above, on the shelves, stands an instant pantry of preserves and dried pulses, rice and pasta, coffee and teas.

All good cooks' kitchens have this sense of an ordered way of life linked to the changing seasons. Onto the kitchen table comes all the produce from the year-round vegetable and herb garden just outside the double-fronted glass doors, either to pass straight from garden to pan, or to be preserved in glass jars on open shelves. Above the table, an overhead galley of storage baskets and cooking pots makes it easy to transfer the contents from one to the other. Tuscan traditions survive: ropes of onions and garlic hang by the cook's chopping board, basil and chervil sprout from pots on a sunny table, shallow baskets hold tomatoes dried to impart their sun-warmed flavour to sauces and soups. Bottles of cold-pressed olive oil scented with basil are lined up by the hob, logs and dried lavender are stacked under the hearth for scented winter fires to warm the kitchen and adjoining dining room.

Plenty of chairs are drawn up around the central table, which becomes a cloth-covered breakfast table or scrubbed work station, or simply a place to sit around and gossip with a cup of mid-morning coffee or a freshly pressed fruit juice. As kitchens lose their glossy-fronted facades on expensive cabinetry to return to being unaffected places for recreation, relaxation and entertaining, this homely place is where the hearth is.

In it, there are hints of country kitchens from all over the world, with punched tinware from Mexico, French enamelled coffee pots, Provencal bowls and Austrian napkins. The rituals of food preparation are associated with pleasure and generosity and this friendly room captures the essence of that bountiful feeling. Its visual delights are as direct and nourishing as the uncomplicated regional recipes which Tricia Guild cooks and shares in the third part of this book. Here is a place designed to encourage good cooking, with fresh produce, whether homegrown or shopped and homemade.

A shelf ranged with jars and bottles in which the scents and flavours, colours and textures of the summer kitchen garden and autumn orchard are distilled is mouth-wateringly appealing to look at, besides being an efficient place to conserve seasonal produce. Tasting the sunwarmed tomato paste on pasta or the pungent peppers preserved in oil is a reminder of sunnier times. When nearby shops are few and far between, or when you have had the good fortune to have a glut of summer vegetables, it can become the most satisfying revelation to open one of these jars. Always keep ready at hand the essentials for cooking.

The shelves were copied from one found in a local junk shop. Their round wooden pegs and scrolled brackets attractively combine the practical with the decorative. Open shelves are the place in this kitchen for bottled fruits, homemade preserves and oils that are labelled and put away like fine wines to mature. Fabric circles cut from swatches are tied with plaid ribbons onto the lids of glass jars filled with dried beans and lentils, the basic ingredients of nourishing winter soups and stews.

Its informal, homespun appearance belies the careful planning that went into this powerhouse, the true heart of this Tuscan home. Arms' reach storage makes for greater efficiency as well as decorative display. The continuing colour theme of slate grey-green on skirting, gates and window surrounds unites the disparate elements within the room, a muted background for the brilliant yellows, reds and greens of flowers and fresh produce in various states of preparation on every surface. The hard tiled floor and stone worktop, cool to the touch on burning summer days, are easy surfaces from which to sweep the debris of chopping, coring and peeling. Sunlight and scents from the garden flood in through double glass doors let into the old stone arched entrance of the farmhouse, whilst the small, deeply-recessed windows are cool and dark to protect volatile cooking ingredients. Metal utensils hang from the shelves; rush baskets hold fresh produce and, on shelves under the worktop, house cutlery and kitchen gadgets; glass and ceramic bowls and storage jars stand within easy reach. This relaxed but functional working environment is dedicated to the production of good, nutritious food for the well-being of family and friends.

# THE VEGETABLE & HERB GARDEN

The kitchen opens onto this terrace where breakfasts of cappuccino, yoghurt and honey, apricots and peaches are taken. Down the stone steps leading to the vegetable garden comes all the harvested produce for use in the house. The floor of the terrace is made from pebble-studded cement inlaid with terracotta-tiled diamonds and squares to define distinct areas for seating and eating. Borders bring a sense of order to open spaces. In the vegetable garden, low box hedge borders also separate and protect the plants.

Since temperatures plummet in winter, low stone walls shelter the whole area. The garden is reached through two arbours. The planting plan of this area so close to the house has been directed with colour in mind, rows of tomatoes and nasturtiums, red peppers and strawberries massed in tones of crimson in one area, separated by trimmed box hedges from the blue area, where borage and sage mingle with peas clambering up little sticks. Lemon-scented geranium and lavender scent the mid-summer air amid banks of green herbs that are clipped to add to soups and salads, basil to flavour oils and rosemary and thyme to spike roasting vegetables.

Herbs and vegetables are planted in successive waves to ensure a steady supply throughout the summer. Early in the season, wisteria and clematis shade the gravel paths dividing the beds of young tender vegetables; later, nasturtiums trail amongst the plants providing crimson and orange flowers and spicy young leaves to flavour summer salads.

# LEMON YELLOW BEDROOM

Despite the attractions of garden and countryside outside, Tricia Guild has created bedrooms you never want to leave, each one as individual and full of character as its inhabitants. There is pattern everywhere — even white bed linen has embroidered borders in giddy polka dots or scallops — but the background of stone and brick floors, painted walls and whitewashed ceilings is uninterrupted. The mood is serene and peaceful. Lemon, lime, aquamarine and pink sharpen up the senses in this idyllic guest bedroom, with its iron bedstead painted verdigris and adorned with a patterned quilt in all the colours of a bed of Icelandic poppies. White linen with yellow checked pillowslips and shocking pink and yellow taffeta cushions make the queen-sized bed both comfortable and comforting. Reddened wood neatly frames a pair of botanical prints against a lemon backdrop. The tiled floor is brightened with simple blue and yellow striped rag rugs placed just where you alight from the bed, a thoughtful touch on a cold hard floor. Large-scale, mismatched old furniture introduces simply the theme of rusticity.

In contemporary interiors it is the mix, not the match, that makes a room work. In this bedroom all the basic pieces are quite individual, from the bed to the all important closet, an old linen press or armoire.

It is important when composing rooms to follow some basic rules, one of which is to balance and contrast the size of furniture: never let one piece outshine all the others. Whether it is by means of colour or size, play one piece against another. To something dark, add a flash of light; next to something massive and square such as this armoire, juxtapose a small sculptural piece like the chair. This is the real key to mixing, not matching which is blandly anonymous.

Proportion is the geometry of space and in this square room with its tiny windows the large armoire, functional as well as a focal point in the centre of the room, is in proportion to the length and breadth of the bed and to the size of the windows and doors. Like the single yellow daisy afloat in a jagged-toothed platter, this exaggerated disproportion draws instant attention to itself, far more pleasing and unexpected than the classical notion of perfect symmetry. A sense of proportion allows you to exaggerate the size of objects, or the scale between various elements, to accentuate or disguise their differences.

In its original state this house was not connected to running water, so space was carved out within every bedroom area for an adjoining bathroom, each carefully sited so that runaway pipes are not visible from the outside. Every one of these small bathrooms continues the colour and pattern theme of its adjacent bedroom — here a painted border of diamond-studded lime green and pink stripes runs around the doors and walls of both rooms — and maintains the tiled floors and colourwashed plaster walls of the rest of the house. Almost monastic in their simplicity, with white pedestal basins and hard floors, the addition of little indulgences such as sweet-smelling soaps, flowers and freshly laundered towels turns necessity into a pleasure.

In a large house where there are many changes of palette and direction, the space between major rooms becomes an important sequential link. These transitional spaces, the doorways, lintels and window sills set in thick walls that gently introduce these changes, must interact to introduce the colours of the rooms on either side and filter the flow from one vibrant scheme to another.

This upstairs landing connecting the main blue bedroom with two guest bedrooms, one graphically coloured in black and white, the other in lemon and lime, has narrow doorways at either end and a pair of small windows over-looking a balconied terrace. The entrance at one end is coloured with broad green stripes on the white walls, at the other in broad bands of indigo. Thus two strong colours, blue and green, introduce the shift in colour emphasis from one area to another.

The original Tuscan window within thick stone outer walls is shown open (left) and closed (right) to reveal small green shutters folded back against the recessed walls, painted meridian blue to filter the light. The ladder-backed wooden bench picks up on this blue and green theme in a sharper palette of turquoise over lime, which lightens up an otherwise solid wooden piece. The roughly scumbled and distressed finish of the paintwork makes a bold contrast with the solid blocks of colour on the walls and at the windows. A woollen throw woven by Richard Wormesley both softens the lines of the bench and introduces a pleasing patterned effect to the decorative scheme.

In some areas, such as this impromptu resting place, flowers can introduce a totally fresh look within a boldly coloured frame. Flowers add variety, mood and emphasis amidst surroundings that remain static and this small nosegay is framed as vividly as any painting. Just as the colours of the little posy are carefully related to the strength of its blue surround, the size and container also relate to the shape of the window: a tall, thin window, for example, would have called for a strong vertical emphasis with a tall vase of long stemmed flowers.

Beyond this landing, out of doors, is a little first floor terrace reached by stone stairs clustered with terracotta pots and old olive jars filled with pink and red geraniums.

# COBALT BEDROOM

Everybody has an individual response to strong colour; the use of it is the ultimate example of self expression. The main bedroom in this house is the embodiment of Tricia Guild's style. Walls are anchored between whitewashed raftered ceiling and terracotta flagged floor by a strong cobalt blue and the monochromatic theme continues in the furnishings. There are no florals and few patterns in the room except for geometric checks, plaids and stripes. The liveliness comes from the steadfast, sure, confident application of colour — an amazing feat in a single colour room which runs through a variety of shades to encompass indigo, cornflower, turquoise, cobalt and morning glory in all its hues. The blue notes are played like jazz, with repeated chords and groupings, sometimes solo like the sky-blue plaid on the ottoman tempered with rhythmic bands of white. Like the friendly posy of freshly picked flowers in the majolica jug, where morning glory's purpling blooms are tempered by spikes of delphinium, blues of the same tonal quantity in exaggerated disproportion vividly enliven the room.

These walls were painted deep blue in line with Tricia Guild's predilection for concentrating the darkest value of a colour on the largest area of a room. The success of introducing other colours depends upon the analogous colours such as blue and green or pink and orange. A toning scheme, made up of a combination of the colours that lie closest to each other in the spectrum, is enlivened by accent colours, like the yellow and green in the crackly silk taffeta curtains tied back with a twist of blue fabric, or the pink piano keynote pattern painted onto the blue band that runs around the room at skirting board height. A monochrome room with many variations on a single theme needs these small accents distributed around it in proportion to its shape and size. It is the balance of colour that creates energy within a space.

Using the blue in different tones and on different textures creates unusual effects. On plastered walls, cotton plains or woven woollen throws, ceramics with all the blues of Chinese and Mexican porcelain and on paper, cotton or silk, the blues take on different tones. Even wood is treated as a colour, rubbed with paint. The smoothed glow of the terracotta flagstone floor acts as a solid base colour to underpin all these shades of blue. Floor and walls may be in the background but with these large areas so boldly defined, they animate the room.

The rectangular pattern of the slabbed floor set at a diagonal gives a sense of expanding space in this large, dark room. Though the windows are small, the imaginative use of monochromatic strong blue actually accentuates the contrasting brightness, stressing light and medium values. The dazzling intensity of blues is highlighted at the windows, where aquamarine, lime and yellow with emerald challenge nature's basic landscape of blue and green. Although successfully paired in nature, within the confines of a room green needs to be used in exactly the right amount to balance blue. Here, bright emerald and sharp green in crinkly silk taffeta appear to draw the light inwards through the small windows to filter out its heat, while bringing that exuberant light into the innermost recesses of the cool blue room.

Window dressing affects the entire mood of a room. Curtains are more than merely decoration: in hot climates they are a practical way to deflect the light, whilst in cold climates, interlined and drawn, they are better than double glazing on cold nights. On these windows, yellow and green taffeta plaid is flounced over white linen banners, tempering the unbroken areas of white and illustrating how colours work together. Where the indigo and emerald weave crosses the flamboyant yellow silk threads, the colours turn aquamarine and sea-blue. Tied onto iron curtain rings that run on iron rods, these banners soften the lines of the tiny energy-efficient windows. They can be hooked up and swathed into simple swags along the curtain pole, or caught at sill height with a twist of contrasting fabric to fall upon the hard floor. Although simple, they are glamorous.

Despite the turn of the century fruitwood furniture and antique iron bedstead, this is a room of clean, uncluttered modernity which establishes that paradox of matched, but not really matched, colours and materials. Painting the walls in several shades of the same colour creates an illusion of a different world beyond, of layered colour and a patina of age that the bold banding in pink and green brings up to date. Vivid blues such as the indigo and cobalt that bring depth to the background give way to gentler, subtler lavenders and turquoises, in turn superseded by stronger, sharper combinations of blue and green. Only the walls beneath the windows and the radiators, carefully positioned there for the best ventilation, are painted white to hold the light. White is the perfect foil for blue. Reflecting the colours and light around it, white takes on many hues. At noon, in this blue room, these areas of white become almost lavender; at dawn, pale turquoise and, at dusk, they darken to a purple haze. White is seldom white, except on a grey day.

Occupying by far the largest amount of space in the room (and the main purpose for it) the bed must be carefully dressed to tone in with the room but not to dominate it. The iron bedstead is painted black and verdigris. White embroidered sheets and pillow slips are covered by several lengths of checked and plain blue or blue-and-white fabric, which make effective counterpanes. The day bed at the foot of the iron bedstead is upholstered in a blue-and-white stripe, edged with braid and a feathery fringe. The tailored look is softened and loosened up with the addition of comfortably plump cushions in various fabrics and a plaid blanket pulling in all the other colours distributed around the room.

Lime green and white stripes link the bedroom with its en suite bathroom, tucked around the corner for privacy. With its theme of blue-and-white checks, this room, too, takes its inspiration from the swirling blue Tuscan sky. A sharp little lime border around the basin and marble bath surround reflects the fields of broom viewed from the window.

# THE UPSTAIRS SITTING ROOM

This group of day bed, upholstered chair, wooden bench and a pair of farmhouse chairs makes an inviting conversation point where people gather to read, talk or play backgammon. Sited between main and guest bedrooms at the top of the stairs, the cosy landing space was the main living room of the original farmhouse. It still retains the deep hearth which was the only source of heat and on which all meals were cooked.

Few sights do more to restore well-being than flowers indoors. Here, the simplest containers are filled, not with grand florists' bouquets, but with the simple pickings from a country border. Nasturtium's golden trumpet, a hosta, a pink geranium, a crimson zinnia and the sharp lime of tolomeia resolve their differences in line and colour to catch the eye. These two posies in lime and turquoise pots on a café table reflect the distribution of colour around the room. There are no rules to say which combinations work best together, only an unaffected celebration of what the garden has to offer at that particular time of year.

This affinity with nature leads to an understanding of how a broad brush-stroke of red works alongside an emerald stripe on an outdoor table, just as in this little group a vivid lime green buttoned-back ottoman sits happily in a room in company with a speckled navy and white table, pale washed sky-blue chairs and an aquamarine cupboard.

The upholstered and painted furniture is a good example of how colour is used throughout the house. Vivid geometric plaids or checked fabrics contrast with the roughly painted wooden table and the cupboard, overscaled to dominate the grouping, takes the eye upwards from the seating. On the armoire, strongly saturated and contrasting colours are combined with inset panels in pale turquoise to dazzling effect. The panels are delineated with a sharp lime green border, a detail every bit as strong as the spikes of lime green tolomeia in the vase of flowers. The important thing is to keep a sense of proportion: bear in mind not only the scale of the rooms in which flowers are to be displayed, but also the scale of the containers. Rather than bunch flowers, it is often better to divide them between several different containers, just one or two flowers or leaves in each, with trailing foliage to lengthen the display.

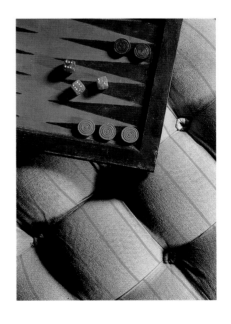

# FLOWERED BEDROOM

By June, drifts of yellow amidst sharp green colour the Tuscan landscape as the wild broom flowers. Once again, the countryside provides the inspiration for a vivid scheme in a guest bedroom, where golden yellows with lime green and blue borders evoke summer all year round. The way in which large-scale pieces of mismatched furniture like the iron bedstead and the armoire are painted pulls them together in harmony and makes the most of these old country pieces. The straight-legged little chair scumbled in blues, green and yellows also looks more interesting in such mixed company.

Built-in closets were only invented in the nineteenth century and prior to that movable storage was provided by chests of drawers or these armoires, traditionally used for linen as well as clothes. An armoire makes a distinguished period piece for a room without closets and is more appropriate in a country bedroom. Their good lines and entablature above the doors are both sensuous and simple, as are the curlecued flourishes on the iron bedstead. By adding a modern mattress covered with layers of brilliant patterns and by painting the armoire white and yellow, cumbersome pieces such as these are adapted to contemporary notions of comfort and function.

In a small guest bedroom the bed and the way in which it is dressed will inevitably become the focal point. Careful attention is paid to the bed linen: white linen sheets and pillowslips, their edges embroidered with polka dots or scrolls, are covered with throws and counterpanes in a variety of geometric prints, each carefully folded back to reveal different reverse linings. Here, a white cotton piqué counterpane is covered with a plaid throw. Another runner in strong yellow, fringed in turquoise, counterbalances the yellow gingham cushions.

In this sunny golden bedroom, an exuberant floral print is kept under control with lots of plaids, checks and ginghams. No rose ever bloomed in such a sharp yellow or in spearmint green with charcoal leaves on a fine stripe, but this graphic representation of florals is a typically modern statement. It is intent on escaping the tedium of the ubiquitous archival flower prints that faithfully try to reproduce nature's many-hued flowers on glazed chintz. A further example of this contemporary architectural approach to interior design is the way in which only a small amount of floral pattern is allowed into a room, then rigorously counterbalanced with geometric stripes and bordered with a fringe to introduce an accent colour. Yet another geometric touch is provided by the striped cotton dhurrie by the bed.

The coming of the sweet-scented broom and the fresh spring greens changes the pace of life from winter. This is a room which celebrates the cherished days of summer. The flowering of big tea roses on simple white curtains all but hides the little window set deep in the thick stone wall. From the closet the scent of lavender drifts from dried sprigs tied into little squares, adding to the fabric and enjoyment of life under the whitewashed raftered ceiling. On the little bedside table an inviting collection of books piled under a reading lamp tempts the visitor to linger. Even when the house is alive with stir and bustle, the aroma of coffee pervading it as the sun shines through the window, this peaceful retreat would prove difficult to leave.

# CHEQUERED BEDROOM

Like a photographic print in black and white, this bedroom needed a graphic composition to pull together opposites. The final effect, with its chalky whites and charcoal greys distanced equally from each other, is not as effortless as it may seem. The amount of black versus white has been carefully balanced and the room given further symmetry with a pair of iron beds, each with their own functional bedside light on a single bedside cupboard. White, black and grey, the shades in this bedroom, are difficult to handle: when white is added to other colours they lighten; add grey and they are dulled, while black will make colours richer. So the proportion of all three in this room is important.

What stops the scheme from having too disciplined an approach is the introduction of pink and green, little intravenous shots of colour coursing through the room to jolt all its elements into liveliness. Details such as the houndstooth skirting board panel that exactly matches the pistachio, black and white banded rug also bring it to life. Accent colour needs to be carefully added. Too much and you flatten the scheme, too little and it will be lost. Try blocking out the colourful pointers by putting your fingers over them and see how lifeless the room becomes. This room is the least colourful in the house, but even here there are finely judged touches: pink ties on the curtain heads, pink and green fringes on the counterpanes and fine lines of colour on the borders. Accent colour can be introduced in a room in many simple ways.

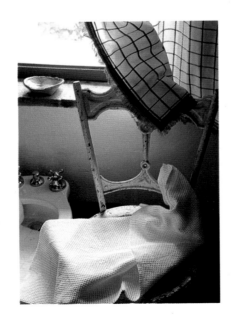

Chalky white and charcoal in this dramatic bedroom show how opposites can attract. The secret to using such a bold treatment lies in the tonal quality of both black and white, as well as in the balance. Change of scale is also important, as in the triangular toothmarked skirting board pattern, inspired by the broad sweep of the cathedral square in Siena. This bold pattern where floor meets white walls is small in scale so that it does not dominate the room and reduce its proportions.

To break up the formality of the black and white, eclectic found furniture is grouped graphically to create a bedroom without walls: the placing of the washstand across a corner of the room produces a diagonal space. A metal folding chair with a portcullis back rest, the bedheads on the single beds and the black and white scrollworked fabric all keep to a strong graphic statement.

White and grey need light to play upon them to break up their direct contrasts. The shutters have been painted olive green in a reference to the framed view of light playing upon the variegated silky grey leaves of olive trees. Notice, too, the influence the soft pink has, not only in the burnished stone of the flagstone floor but also in the fringes edging the bed throws and on the flower bowls. Terracotta pink, shown in close up on flaky old walls, is used here to soften the direct graphic image of black and white. So, too, on the chequerboard tiles running around the entrance to the adjoining bathroom, the black mosaic is held by fine pink line borders.

# GARDEN ROOM

This small outhouse with ivy clambering eagerly up its walls was originally part of the farm. Now sited in mid-garden it has become a private guest bedroom with bathroom and its own little verandah – the perfect shady retreat from the noonday sun. Everything within is chosen to hold and reflect the light, even the pink and yellow plaid on the bed, which in turn suggests the base colours for the patterned cushion covers in spots and stripes. Not much bigger than a single bed in width, the room is brightened even further with walls in two shades of yellow. A lighter underwash shines through the glazed topcoat. The space has a unique character, enhanced by curlecued ironwork on chair, lamp and bedhead, which the two drooping black swans gracefully delineate. The lime and indigo bedside table provides a luminous patch of cool colour, like the soft aquamarine dhurrie on the terracotta floor, itself scoured to a pale smoothness. The furniture has been carefully chosen and positioned in scale to this tiny room.

# THE SUMMER GARDEN

The wooden structure is the only permanent element on this outdoor stage, an infinitely versatile setting for a variety of moods and seasons. An indoor arrangement of cut flowers and leafy clippings on the garden table adds to the outdoor room feeling of this shaded seating area. If a property gives you trees, flowers and fresh produce these are great gifts, but even arid land can be brought back to life as a terrace with shelter and garden furniture. In this garden you can see almost unlimited possibilities for outdoor living, created from nothing other than a patch of ground and a fertile imagination. A shady retreat such as this is simple to make: wooden poles are lashed or nailed to form two attached squares, vines or other climbers obligingly blur the vertical poles and shade is provided by a removable stretch of blue-and-white striped fabric. Straight bricked paths smartly delineate the lines of the pergola on either side whilst carefully placed chairs, a couple of rustic tables and some brightly patterned throws make the group a conversation point.

A solitary bench under the vast spread of an old tree encourages quiet contemplation of the magnificent view and marks the end of Tricia Guild's property on this Tuscan mountainside. Bathed in the midday sunlight, it is easy to see how the garden has clearly been the inspiration for the colour scheme indoors. A hedge of smoky lavender billows along a pink drystone wall in the shade of grey-green olive trees. Here, too, are the sweeps of sunny yellow, the white and the infinite variety of greens. Nature paints on a broad canvas, but it is fascinating to see how these colours can be distilled indoors into intermeshing weaves: indigo and emerald threads crossed in a silk taffeta emerge as aquamarine and turquoise; shocking pink and golden yellow in a plaid turn amber and raspberry. Layers of paint on furniture have different effects — either scumbled so that the colours shine through, or given a crackle glaze to bring patina to the different colours applied below. The result is a magical transformation of nature's colours into a vivid interior scheme.

From this pictorial tour of the house, key elements in the practice of interior design can be observed. Firstly, space: how to define it in harmony with the landscape to blur distinctions between indoors and out. An important aspect of the use of space is the positioning of furniture to allow for traffic flow and to introduce sequential rhythm to the house in the way rooms open out from one another and into the garden. Then, proportion: to interior designers what perspective is to painters, a way of adding depth to rooms by manipulating contrasts in scale. Next, light: both natural and artificial light are harnessed to make the most of cool, shady corners and to allow strong daylight to stream through the windows, with modern lights for special tasks or ambient candlelight for mood. Function: a kitchen that really works for the cook, comfortable seating and beds, sensible bathrooms. Texture: the way in which it can be used to enliven a scheme and create depth and richness of mood, by contrasting silk taffeta with humble linen, cotton with wool, roughly adzed rustic furniture with antiques. And lastly, colour, to make an immediate and lasting impression on the eye, as well as being the easiest, least costly and most daring way in which to transform a room.

# VINEYARD VIEWS

## PRUNED-DOWN SIMPLICITY

This neighbouring stone house on a Tuscan hillside overlooking a vineladen vale is reached by a lengthy climb through tracts of scented wild oreganum. Below the terrace stretch the wheatfields and vineyards and the distant spires of medieval hill houses. The house was uninhabited for twenty-five years, but the young Italian owners were able to use blocks of handcut fieldstone and red tiles from the derelict building on the site to rebuild it in the vernacular style. Walls were rebuilt using mortar mixed with *calce*, or lime, to match the honey-coloured stone. The owners scoured the countryside to find antique tiles, oak beams, doorknobs and a mantel for the living room fireplace.

Both the architecture and the interior design illustrate the art of understatement. The strong lines of the house suggest pruned-down functionalism, which in no way ignores comfort nor appears wasteful. The owners did not want to turn it into a villa or manor house but to retain the simplicity and honesty of the original farmhouse, set about with alcoves and patios, amidst the olive groves, fruit trees and a small vineyard. Their careful and sympathetic approach to the restoration shows in the natural materials used — the stone, brick and plaster of the floors and walls — as well as in the few possessions with which they furnished the house: antique furniture lovingly polished to a soft sheen, the blonde wood kitchen table scoured to the colour of pale straw. An appreciation of natural materials encouraged them to pursue a simplified furnishing scheme.

The pale pumice-stone colours of the interior are enhanced by walls painted a soft pink, which adds depth and softens the austere lines of the architecture. As in many Tuscan houses, a band of colour at skirting board height runs the length of the rooms and up over the lintels on plain stone walls. When planning a decoration scheme, it is important to evaluate what you have and make the most of it. This can be as simple as positioning furniture and objects correctly or providing comfortable seating where it is most needed; it can be a question of decorative detailing with paint, or a quick fabric change. Details such as these can uplift any interior scheme. This is the pared-down approach.

Vernacular architecture dictates the furnishing style: rather than putting in large windows to frame the hilltop view, the owners left the deep-set little windows in place; double doors are painted and folded back from large entrances, allowing continuous access from one room to another; low beams overhead are whitewashed to hold the light, to emphasise the height of the ceiling visually and lighten the room. Thus what is already there is exaggerated and enhanced to decorative effect. In the same way as a painter observes perspective, the natural proportions of this regional house suggest the scheme. Small windows are left unadorned or dressed simply with lengths of fabric tied onto rings. Stone walls and flagstoned floors are left plain. Mismatched sofas, chaise longue and chair form a symmetrical group for relaxed conversation. A plain linen or cotton throw and cushions disguise old upholstery and at the same time add a touch of colour co-ordination, proving that it is not always necessary to spend lavishly on new covers.

The vertical lines of the blue-grey doors are reinforced with a pair of cupboards on either side and furniture is grouped where it is best viewed, framed in the entrance, anchored by the natural sea-grass woven mat. Cherrywood furniture, its gracious lines lovingly polished, brings a certain formality to the house. There are few accessories: walking sticks for country strolls, baskets of logs, candlesticks and vases for flowers. Nothing is here for artifice or show, everything has a use. Making the most of the light streaming in through the small window, a sunny yellow, orange and red banner, bordered in a sharp green, the colour of cantaloupe melons, hangs full length to provide a jolt of pattern and colour. In the kitchen a scrubbed wooden table is a solid, functional background for fresh herbs from the garden, vegetables from the market, lemons plucked from the tree outside and the essential pestle and mortar, where basil, pine nuts and Parmesan are pounded into pesto. Storage is provided by baskets and market boxes, both efficient and inexpensive.

The pressures of life seem far removed from this serene bedroom. Taking a theme is one way of furnishing a room and here it is provided by nature: both the antique bedspread and the botanical watercolours, formally arranged on plaster skim walls, suggest a flowery bedroom that is far from girlish or whimsical. As the bed is the largest area in the room it is a natural focal point to set the scene with a cotton bedspread sprigged with embroidered flowers. This floral tribute is emphasised by cut flowers tucked into plain containers. Simple accessories take the room out of the faded past and into a lively present with pink and white fabrics in a palette inspired by the hibiscus which bursts from deep red buds to reveal powdery pink blooms. Just two colours do the work of a multitude more effectively when used with a soft background. The pink glow of the wall is background to a folding luggage rack, the dressing table and the chest of drawers that, together, evoke another, altogether more restful time, like the whole of this peaceful house.

Sloping eaves and a herringboned floor introduce an interesting pattern as a background to the strongly coloured yellow and red fabrics in this room. The colours of a bold floral curtain carry through to the ochre-yellow bedspread in a plain weave and the coral fringes on white cushions and bedspread. Fabrics introduce colour combinations in a professional way. If in doubt about how to use colour in a room, begin with a patterned fabric predominantly in a preferred colour, then pick out the other colours in this manner. Large surface areas on the walls or floor will harmonise or neutralise the fabric colours, whereas little accent colours on trimming, such as the coral fringes, will emphasise them.

Natural linen is a fabric with texture and an understated simplicity which falls and drops gracefully. Here, a capacious easy chair is entirely swathed in a piece of linen cut generously so that it flounces loosely upon the floor, making a feature of a cumbersome piece of furniture. On well-upholstered pieces, throws work best when tucked into the plump lines of a sofa, across the arms or over the backrest, to inject a change of colour or pattern into a large unbroken area of fabric.

In the adjoining bathroom, a skirt of white linen fringed in coral and white seersucker is gathered around the functional washstand, effectively softening its lines and hiding the plumbing. The best position in the room, beneath the window for the most natural light, is occupied by the bath, made larger by its tiled platform surround.

Antique twin beds, with elegant scrolled bedheads, are redolent of a more formal age and suggest a totally different mood in this bedroom created within the old toolshed of the farmhouse. In style with their period feel, the beds are covered in crimson and claret and dressed with pillows and bolsters. An old Paisley throw softens the severity, just as the golden and crimson checked curtain brightens the dark silks and sparks them into life. In this small, dark room with its heavy period furniture the strong light catching the fiery shades of colour to make them glow is an important element in its success. A dark scheme in a predominantly dark room will only work if brought to life with judicious use of accent colours. Here, they are provided by the painted cupboard, its red panels inset in ambered frames against golden walls, by red poppies framed by the green shutter on the window sill and by the white pillows, deliberately left out under the bolsters on the beds. The tiny bathroom, its natural stone and wood enhanced by shades of buttermilk and white, provides a cool retreat from the summer heat.

# RUSTIC FARMHOUSE

## THINK NATURALLY — TAKE A LEAF FROM NATURE

Atop another nearby hill in Tuscany, this reassuringly stolid, handsome house is well crafted and comfortably furnished. It sums up the new attitude to think naturally, a resourceful resolution to making a family home out of an old farmhouse. Regional architecture offers not only practical, but natural, design solutions. In common with many old houses, it was built to take advantage of local materials and climatic conditions; once warmed, its thick stone walls retain the heat of open fires in winter; in summer, they maintain a cool temperature within, providing a respite from the outdoor heat. Small windows set into the thick stone walls let in enough strong light whilst cooling the air which pervades the house. A home such as this needs to be furnished with a few basics: comfortable seating around occasional tables positioned near windows to get the most daylight or near the hearth to draw warmth on wintry nights. Realizing early on that this handsome vernacular architecture needs little adornment, the owners furnished it sparingly with a few good pieces of local furniture, avoiding clutter.

This house has been rebuilt with a sense of purpose and a strong feel for architectural space. The mood and feel of both restoration and decoration is rustic, in keeping with the spirit of these Tuscan farmhouses. The interior is restored with local materials and painted with soft colours derived from the Renaissance artist Piero della Francesca. The windows, in natural tones of stone and wood, frame the beauty of the surrounding countryside. In harmony with this pared-down approach, the walls are roughly whitewashed and the regular slabbed stone floors scrubbed and left bare. In places, the original blocks of honeyed stone are allowed to show through the later plasterwork, bringing an honest, crafted feel to the place. The traditional Tuscan painted border is the only interior paint effect, this time in a soft sage green.

The choice of fabrics in this house reflects the subdued natural palette of stone and terracotta, brick and wood. Curtains, tablecloths and bed linen, occasional cushion covers, throws and bedspreads are simple and discreet so as not to spoil the laid-back charm of the setting. The result looks settled, a lovingly preserved piece of the past.

Old country kitchens, alive with stir and bustle and the aroma of delicious dishes being prepared and cooked, have a lesson to teach those who think good food is synonymous with expensive kitchen styling. Apart from a cooker, a kitchen needs sensible storage and functional working surfaces. This kitchen makes a feature of everything it contains, as well as keeping it all close to hand. On top of the range, pans and pots bubble, whilst hung around it are all the essential cook's utensils such as ladles, sieves and spoons. The curvaceous stone worktop, which stays as cool as an old farm dairy, supports baskets of fresh local produce and houses the double sink unit. On the wall a decorative wrought iron rack displays freshly laundered tea towels, their checks echoed by the diagonal runner on the table. Provisions are mainly stored in the nearby walk-in pantry, one of the other advantages of an old house, but they could just as easily be lined up in jars and bottles on the worktop or on bracketed shelves. Above all, it is a companionable place, with a sense of space and continuity.

The adjoining dining room maintains the neutrals on walls, floors and raftered ceiling, warmed up with rich chestnut and fruitwood furniture. It is more formal than the kitchen both in its grouping and in the elegant pieces, such as the three turn-of-the-century chairs with scroll-like arms set upon curvaceous legs, contrasting with the straightbacked dining chairs pulled up around the polished table. A huge cupboard with multi-panelled doors makes a focal point on an exaggerated scale behind the dining table. From there, the eye is drawn to the trestle-legged table and the naive painting of a bowl of cherries above the tabletop baskets of fresh leaves and food. So, changes of scale enhance the proportions within a room. Vivid lime with turquoise throws and a lime and white linen runner energise the room and reinforce the feeling of formality, without overdressing what is still a farmhouse room. In a different mood, the terrace features plain country furniture and a casual fringed cloth, an informal spot to retreat into the shade illuminated by a brightly coloured child's painting.

The amount of colour used in a furnishing scheme is as important as the colours themselves. In this room, the surrounding countryside has been a natural influence upon the choice of colours, sky blue and green from the vines on the wooded hillside. Outside, green predominates, but inside, blue holds the dominant note on the low squat table below the window, the two ornately plaited wicker chairs and a moody blue painting which is almost as big as the window. Contrasting greens appear on the checked cushions on the chairs and on two small unlined curtains simply tied to the curtain rail. Fussy and pretentious furnishings have no place in this house and the two brightly coloured little curtains highlight the limited use of fabric. The strong but plain and functional architectural background does not need more than some cushions and curtains, some pots and bowls.

In a quiet corner of the sitting room an ancient boulder has been allowed to burst through the white plaster walls. Around this natural evidence of the hillside to which the house clings is a group of old clay olive pots and one giant olive jar, themselves reminders of the land which provided the inhabitants' livelihood. Against this rustic background the two pieces of furniture, a simple wooden table and an old reclining steamer chair, are brightened by sunny yellow plaids and sunflowers. The warm colours of apricots and zinnias in crimson, scarlet and magenta bring to life the natural finishes within the neutral space.

Elegance and ease are two difficult goals to bring together in a furnishing scheme. The key is to seek the best quality. This does not necessarily depend on the amount of money spent but on an understanding of classic design and good lines, such as these wicker chairs, the slatted wooden recliner and handsome fruitwood occasional chairs. Classics earn their reputation on the back of workmanlike usefulness coupled with a simplicity of line. Good craftsmanship and honest materials signal classic design.

These raftered bedrooms have no need of frills. The natural fibres of cotton and linen hang easily against unadorned woods. The golden clay floor and roughly plastered walls are an admirable backdrop for a few pieces of classic furniture: the solid armoire, marble-topped chest of drawers and blanket box for simple storage combine necessity and frugality with a certain style. Few colour mixes are as appealing and as natural as blue and white, but whereas Tricia Guild has used blue over the large areas of her bedroom, here the reverse is the case. White walls, white counterpane and white marble top lighten the effect of the large dark armoire which dominates the room. Blue polka dots and checks on the bed linen and the blue scrolled pattern tumbling in repeats upon white drops at the window and on the throw over the bed introduce a joyful note to the room. The tiny, shuttered windows of the adjoining bathroom are simply hung with crushed white linen banners to filter the piercing rays of bright sunlight. Minimal, without being modern, these rooms are satisfying in their simplicity.

# A HILLTOP HOUSE

## LOOSEN UP, LET A BANNER CATCH THE BREEZE

A revolution in decoration has taken place behind closed doors, but the idea of decorating out of doors is entirely new. When the weather is warm, a life without walls invites us to venture outside. In her own home, Tricia Guild has shown how to make innovative use of fabric awnings in the garden. At a friend's house nearby, she demonstrates how to loosen up for outdoor, and indoor, living in ways that will encourage you to use every centimetre of your property.

A great outdoor room can be a place to call home for the summer. To create one is simply a matter of making ingenious use of the space available, by tying up metres of summery fabric from a pole or homemade pergola, or even from the corners of a balcony or poles used for a washing line in the city. All good ideas travel well and are adaptable, as well as value-conscious.

This hilltop house, ringed with woodland, has the old bleached skeleton of a timber outhouse standing outside the kitchen door, a reminder of things past. All it needed was some awnings hung over the roof and banners at either end to turn it into a summerhouse and some simple furniture to make it a place for eating or relaxing. Beneath the blue-and-white striped chaise longue are the bare bones of an old recliner, too weatherbeaten to be enjoyed until dressed; cloth draped casually over the wooden table creates a focal point in the shelter, expressed in the humblest materials. Despite their random appearance, the choice of materials is studied. Fabric pieces are each cut deliberately to different lengths and widths to bring interest to the building, making a casual awning rather than an exactly measured attempt to fill the space. The use of blue and white as the colour scheme counters the green of the surroundings, echoing the hot blue sky and the cool blues of the paintwork on shutters and furniture.

A collection of fabric pieces, like these lengths of fringed white calico and the simply tied blue and white scrollwork banners, is easily rolled and stored at the end of summer. With them, your outside space can be transformed for the summer, sitting rooms and bedrooms can be given a seasonal facelift, a temporary resting place can become an instant home.

This house is a good example of the relaxed, loosened-up approach to decorating for a friendly, undaunting interior. Loosening up means learning from what is already around you. In this case, the position of doors and windows creates a difficult corner in the sitting room, but by exaggerating it with the addition of modular sofas, upholstered with studied frivolity in blue and white gingham, what might have been an awkward space becomes a comfortable focal point. Taking a leaf from nature, a blue and green patterned fabric with a jolt of shocking pink is introduced at the window. This in turn draws attention to the pink band that runs around the windows and the blue stripe at dado height which defines the seating area. The same colours are introduced in the nearby downstairs bedroom, where the flowered curtains sharpen up the soft blues in the room. The pink appears again to line the reverse sides of the blue duvets. Once more, the vernacular use of softly painted borders is used to effect throughout the house, linking the rooms and making a feature of an otherwise plain passageway.

A colourful woollen throw hangs loosely from a row of bent iron coathooks on a painted plaster backdrop. The chalky pastel borders which frame the entrances in this house broaden in the passageway almost to dado height, echoing the honeysuckle colours in the pantry: green, yellow and pink with lots of white. Behind a yellow door, the kitchen brightens up with a striped tablecloth and upholstered window seat. The cool stone butler's sink revives vegetables which are stored in baskets and well-stocked provisions are tidily housed. With rush-seated wooden chairs and stools around a solid farmhouse table it is as if time has stood still for centuries in this functional room. Marble, stone and tiles are ideal cold surfaces for the storage and preparation of food in a hot area which until recently had no fridges or freezers in which to preserve perishables, but their hard lines are softened with patterned fabrics and vivid cotton cushions.

The scarlet poppy's face suggests the colour theme for this cheerful bedroom, tucked under the vine-covered eaves with views for ever over the rolling Tuscan countryside. Single beds are painted crimson, their tall canopies simply draped with white awnings tied with a twist of red braid. A painterly flowered fabric is used as a counterpane, its striped borders like strewn poppy petals in a pattern that is anything but overblown.

To use colours to good effect it is necessary to understand the backup colours: a yellow square in a white frame will appear smaller. Tone also changes, so that yellow in a white surround appears lemony, but in a black surround seems as hot and vibrant as sunflowers. A strong colour such as red should be tempered with lots of white. In this room, little bits of red are scattered all about so that the vivid colour is not all focussed on one large item such as the bed. Red and white striped lampshades and a bunch of poppies and other wild flowers in a glass jar on the shared bedside table make the point.

The success of using such a dazzling shade of colour depends on marshalling it. Here, this is done with crimson uprights on the bedframe and the painted line running across the walls at pillow height. Just as the golden border frames the view, the red line of the bed uprights frames the pattern of the fabrics.

# MEDITERRANEAN BLUES

## SEASCAPE COLOURS DAZZLE IN A GREEK ISLAND VILLA

All the colours of the Aegean Sea, from blue to jade green where the sea hits a sunlit patch of sand, are reflected in this luminous house. Strong blue drenches the walls, the fireplace surround, even the stair treads, to prove that safe magnolia or cream or ivory walls have no place in today's contemporary interiors. Style is expressed through colour. Putting colour onto large areas like walls, floors and ceilings and then co-ordinating the furnishings is the basis for all home decoration. Colours can be matched, contrasted or highlighted with paints, papers and fabrics to create both mood and style, to change proportion and to lighten space. Colours themselves are changed by other colours and by the light through which they are seen. Under the dazzling white light of a Greek island, deep blue intensifies and glows, showing up the heat whilst keeping it cool, and does not fall into sombre shadows as it would in colder northern lights. The use of this strong blue throughout the house is tempered with complementary colours such as lime green, turquoise and emerald green. White is also used as a colour here; with so much blue and fuchsia and shocking pink it is vibrant, stimulating the intensity of the other colours.

This simple stone house sums up the pared-down, natural look that Tricia Guild loves so much, but here in this eastern Mediterranean setting there are differences. Whereas in the soft, rolling countryside of Tuscany exterior walls are left in their natural stone to blend with the earthy colours of the surroundings, here in the starker, bleached Greek island setting they are painted white to reflect the sparkling light from sea and sky. High walls, arches and courtyards provide areas of vital shade at different times of day, as well as places for sun-loving plants to thrive in terracotta pots. Inside, windows are kept tightly shuttered against the heat and even fabric and furnishings are kept to a bare minimum to make the most of the cool air generated by thick stone floors and walls. In this arid landscape, all the necessities of life must be culled from the sea or the dry earth. The strong light seems to bring out an intensity of colour everywhere, from the sun-ripened vegetables and fruits which appear daily in the markets to the painted patterns on locally made ceramic bowls and jugs.

Pattern holds the floor in this house, with traditional cobbles in the living area and cement, painted blue, used in the passageways. The most decorative aspect of the casual sitting room is the pebbled floor, with its geometric scroll-like border. Being the largest area, this patterned space becomes the focal point. Vibrant cushions are scattered on citrus lime mattresses against the wall, the odd pieces of furniture painted blue and outlined in bright crimson. In common with most old Mediterranean homes, every item in the house has its function. In the sitting room a studded chest provides the only storage as well as a low surface for lanterns and candlesticks. Apart from one chair, with its attendant footstool, seating is at floor level around the simple legless wooden table. The walls are hung throughout with functional objects: iron coat hooks in the passage, wooden racks holding painted earthenware plates in dining room and kitchen. Patterned fabric in the sitting room provides the only touch of decoration on the walls.

Checked and striped fabric banners at the deep-set window filter the bright light into a myriad colours around this alcove bedroom. The yellow and white duvet cover emphasises the joyful, sunny feeling of the room, whilst the choice of mismatching checks and stripes gives it an air of informal comfort. By night, the drapes of turquoise, green and gold silk taffeta are drawn to shimmer in candlelight, darkening and changing the mood entirely. The use of silks and taffetas against plain stone and wood, as well as the positive colours, can dictate the entire character of a room: nowhere more important than in a bedroom, place of rest, relaxation and dreams.

Dark rich tones of blue are teamed with wood and lightened only by white and an enlivening touch of red. The introduction of little accent colours, such as the yellow glass, the golden wicks in lanterns, daisies and wild flowers in a jug, are touches that bring the whole scheme to life.

The overall effect in all these houses is of fresh and original interiors that exhibit comfort without excess, and show an individual style which can be put into practice anywhere by following the simple maxims: *think natural, pare down, loosen up, colour in* and *live well.*

# LIVING & ENTERTAINING

## ENJOYING THE FRUITS OF THE COUNTRYSIDE

The joy of country living is the ability to bring the outside in, to fill your house with the flowers and greenery of the garden and hedgerows and to eat what is produced in your region. For Tricia Guild, this means enjoyment of the fresh produce of the Tuscan countryside, an appreciation of seasonal foods homegrown or bought in local markets, presented for family and friends on colourful plates and platters on her boldly painted tabletops or on linen laundered and crisp with napkins, with pitchers of cool drinks and glasses, fresh flowers and leaves in pots. The following pages show how fresh garden produce can be prepared, cooked and served to look and taste its best.

The Italian diet, with its emphasis on pasta and rice, vegetables and salads prepared with fresh-pressed olive oil, plenty of fish and few dairy products, is healthy as well as delicious. But you don't have to live in Italy to follow the same simple philosophy of eating seasonally what is provided by the countryside around you. Part of living well is to be generous with the best ingredients and time. The garden or the greengrocer is a constant reminder of the passing months; as each new root or leaf or fruit makes its appearance, so a dish that is right for the moment suggests itself. Even the winter can be enjoyed with stored beans and pulses, winter fruit compotes and preserves made from a late summer glut.

Freshly-picked fruits and vegetables need only the simplest preparation for their distinct flavours to be released and enjoyed to the full. Light and tasty dishes such as artichokes with mint and lemon, pasta with broccoli and pine nuts, pears with pecorino cheese, homemade ice cream with a fruit coulis, are pleasing to the eye as well as the palate, their fresh natural colours shown off to advantage with colourful plates and napkins. Menus such as these are proof, too, that green doesn't have to be boring.

Living well is about the creative aspect of growing, cooking and presentation. It's an attitude of mind rather than an extravagance. Above all, it's the quality that comes from caring. Spontaneity and generosity are more a part of it than planning ahead. Sharing freshly home-baked bread and sliced tomatoes and basil from the garden with a friend can be as satisfying as an elaborately prepared meal.

Punctuate your garden with places to sit, to take in the view, to pause quietly for a while. Make space for tables — in a shady area under trees, on a terrace or surrounded by colourful or scented plants.

The best-dressed tables mix things: take blue and white as a theme, mixing splatter with formal polka dots, French marbled china, Italian rustic ceramics in matching or complementary colours or textures. For a relaxed meal out of doors this cloth, hand-embroidered by Lisa Vaughan, covers a painted wooden table, the fresh petalled background to bowls and plates with a jug of flowers and aromatic herbs picked straight from the garden — spontaneous, but it's a success because there is a theme and the colours work together.

### ARTICHOKES WITH MINT AND LEMON

Take 12 small fresh artichokes. Cut off the tops and remove the outer leaves down to the tender green inner leaves. Shave and cut off the stems, leaving approx 50mm/2in. Rub with lemon juice and set aside. Chop 50g/2oz each fresh mint and flat-leaved parsley, 2 cloves garlic, mix together with a little salt and rub around the artichokes.

Place the artichokes heads down in a heavy-based pan, add 2 halved lemons and a mixture of water and oil (two-thirds water to one-third oil) just to cover them. Cover with a lid, bring to the boil and cook gently for approx 40 minutes until soft. Test with a fork. Serve warm or at room temperature sprinkled with mint.

Red and white checks make a bold background for a jug of yellow wild flowers mixed with rosemary, and pots of basil ready to impart their peppery flavour when the leaves are added to soups and tomato sauces. Red, yellow and green peppers and two varieties of tomato, grown as much for their beauty as their sun-ripened flavour, are displayed with fresh salad leaves in a trio of baskets. Tomatoes, a few colourful peppers, some marinated local olives and freshly baked bread create a light al fresco lunch. When roasted, skinned and soaked in olive oil, these strips of pepper show off their bright colours against a background of many blues, a tin can at the ready to drizzle on yet more thick, aromatic olive oil. A runner of red-striped linen is the perfect table covering to set off fresh tomatoes and bruschetta, pieces of grilled Italian bread rubbed with garlic and olive oil, that are the basis of impromptu lunches in the garden. They can be served with a variety of cheese or vegetarian toppings.

### ROASTED PEPPERS IN OLIVE OIL

Roast peppers in a hot oven for about 30 minutes depending on size. They should be slightly burnt on the outside. When cooked, put them immediately into a plastic bag and seal. The skins should now come off easily when cool. Slice the skinned peppers thinly, cover in olive oil, season and add a sprinkling of chopped parsley and garlic. Arrange in a dish in a pattern of coloured strips.

### OLIVE OIL AND GARLIC BRUSCHETTA

To make bruschetta, toast slices of Italian bread. Rub with garlic and salt, drizzle with olive oil and serve warm.

### TOMATO AND BASIL BRUSCHETTA

In advance, roughly chop 8 plum tomatoes, tear 10 basil leaves and crush 1 clove garlic. Mix together, season with salt and freshly ground black pepper, cover with olive oil and keep cool until needed. Spoon over hot bruschetta.

### HERB BRUSCHETTA

In advance, chop about 75g/3oz flat-leaved Italian parsley. Mix with 6 drained anchovy fillets, 1 tbspn drained and chopped capers, ½ chopped dried chilli, 1 clove crushed garlic and season. Cover with olive oil and keep cool until needed. Spread on hot bruschetta and serve immediately.

### TOMATO, MOZZARELLA AND ANCHOVY BRUSCHETTA

Arranged slices of tomato and mozzarella cheese (preferably buffalo mozzarella) on hot bruschetta. Top with anchovy fillets and basil leaves. Add salt and drizzle with olive oil, then serve immediately.

# SUMMER SOUPS

Summer soups made from the freshest, lightly cooked vegetables, served hot or cold, can be dressed up with a sprig of their own leaves or flowers or with a complementary herb. In the case of tomatoes this must be basil, the strongly-scented annual which marries so well with their flavour. Clambering alongside blue borage to spice summer salads, basil grows thick and green to flavour summer. The first zucchini flowers can be deep-fried after lightly coating in batter, or used to adorn summer salads, leaving others to produce the first chartreuse-coloured zucchini for summer soups flavoured with sage, chervil and thyme. In early summer, young shoots of asparagus, still slightly crunchy from very light cooking, taste wonderful drizzled with a little olive oil and scattered with shavings of fresh Parmesan.

### FRESH TOMATO AND BASIL SOUP

Sauté 2 tbspns olive oil, 1 chopped onion and 1 chopped potato together in a covered saucepan for 20 minutes. Add 1.5kg/3¼lb chopped ripe tomatoes and 500ml/15fl oz vegetable stock and simmer for a further 10 minutes. Mouli or blend with fresh basil, season and serve warm or chilled.

### ZUCCHINI SOUP

Sauté 1 chopped medium onion in olive oil, then add 1 sliced small potato and simmer gently in a covered pan for 10 minutes. Roughly slice 1kg/2¼lb zucchini and add to the pan. Just cover with vegetable stock or water and simmer gently for 15-20 minutes, adding 1 handful fresh basil, salt and white pepper. Purée with a medium Mouli blade or blend roughly. Add chopped basil when reheating and serve with a drizzle of olive oil.

# WINTER SOUPS

When winter falls frostily upon the land, root vegetables and the stored goodness of nutritious pulses make warming soups. Winter vegetables also have their complementary seasonal herbs, more strongly flavoured than their delicate summer counterparts. Carrots and coriander seeds, for instance, chick peas with the evergreen rosemary, beans with velvety sage. A warming soup flavoured with fresh herbs and served with crusty hot bread is welcome when winter fires burn. The hot, spicy colours of the flowers, bowls and table linen — saffron, madder, turmeric and shocking pink — are accented by lime green napkins.

### CHICK PEA SOUP

Soak 350g/12oz chick peas overnight, then drain. Sauté 1 chopped large onion, 3 stalks chopped celery and 1 chopped clove garlic in oil for 20 minutes. Add the chick peas and a sprig of fresh rosemary. Cover with chicken or vegetable stock and simmer for 2½-3 hours until the chick peas are really soft. Mouli or blend (reserving a few for garnish), season to taste, then serve with a drizzle of olive oil, garnished with rosemary or chervil and the whole chick peas.

### CARROT SOUP

In a heavy-based pan, heat 2 tbspns olive oil, 1 roughly chopped onion, 8 chopped large carrots, 1 chopped small potato and 12 crushed coriander seeds. Season with salt and pepper, cover and cook gently for 20 minutes. Add vegetable stock to cover, bring to the boil, then simmer for 12 minutes. Mouli or blend, return to the saucepan and heat through. Add fresh coriander, mint or chervil and adjust the seasoning before serving.

### BEAN AND BUCKWHEAT SOUP

Boil 600g/18oz white beans in water for 1-1½ hours until tender. Drain, reserving the cooking water and a few whole beans, then put through a Mouli. Heat some olive oil in a deep saucepan and add 1 chopped onion, 100g/4oz diced pancetta, 1 chopped chilli, 2 stalks chopped celery, 1 grated carrot, 3-4 sage leaves, 1 tsp chopped marjoram and sauté gently. When the onion starts to brown, add 225g/8oz peeled and sieved chopped tomatoes and season. Simmer for 15 minutes, then stir in the bean purée with a little of its own liquid. Mix well, add 150g/5oz *farro* (pre-boiled for 3 hours) or buckwheat (pre-boiled for 1 hour), 500ml/16fl oz vegetable or chicken stock and simmer for 40 minutes. About 10 minutes before the end of this time, add the whole cooked beans and heat through. Serve with a jug of olive oil to add to each bowl.

# BEANS & LENTILS

Beans and lentils are a staple peasant food and an excellent source of nutrition. The subtle, marbled colours and nutty tastes of beans are best appreciated when cooked fresh, but dried, they are a welcome addition to winter soups and casseroles. When using fresh, cook lightly and dress with the best olive oil and a little balsamic vinegar. For winter use, soak dried beans overnight before use, then bring to the boil, cook for 10 minutes and drain, before using in any recipe. This helps to make them more digestible.

Beans are particularly popular in Tuscany, where they grow many varieties. Fagioli are traditionally cranberry beans, pretty in their pink and white marbled shells and pods, but if these are not available dried white beans can be substituted. Fava, or broad beans, are the oldest beans known in Europe. Delicious when fully grown, they can be eaten raw when young or cooked in many ways. Lightly cooked and tossed in olive oil, they are the perfect accompaniment to Parma ham.

### BROAD BEANS

Boil or steam the shelled beans until only just tender so they keep their colour. Drain and season, mix with a little balsamic vinegar and some good olive oil and serve warm or cool either on their own or with Parma ham as a first course, or as a vegetable accompaniment to a main course.

### FAGIOLI

If using dried beans, soak overnight, then drain before use. Bring beans to the boil and cook for 10 minutes. Drain and replace with fresh water. Bring to the boil again and simmer until tender. Strain, then mix with slivers of finely sliced red onion, some good olive oil, salt and pepper and a touch of white wine vinegar. Serve warm or cool, garnished with chopped flat-leaved parsley or mint or sprigs of sage.

## ONION SOUP

Sauté 4 chopped onions and 1 chopped clove garlic in oil until the onions are very soft and starting to colour. Add 1 chopped potato, 2 sprigs rosemary and some vegetable or chicken stock to cover; simmer gently until the potato is cooked. Put this mixture through a Mouli or blend, then reheat, season and stir in a little cream. Serve garnished with fried croûtons.

## LENTIL SALAD

Soak small Puy lentils for 2 hours. Drain, then simmer with 1 small onion and some fresh sage in water for 30-40 minutes until just tender. Strain and leave to cool. Serve tossed with a generous dressing made from olive oil, balsamic vinegar, salt and pepper and a handful of chopped fresh coriander or mint.

# HERBS

Most herbs will grow happily in pots or window boxes or you can now buy them fresh all year round. Always use fresh — dried herbs are a poor substitute, lacking flavour as well as nutritional value. Whenever possible use in handfuls, so that their unique scents and tastes can really pervade the dish.

## HERB PESTO

Traditionally, pesto is made with basil, pine nuts, garlic, pecorino cheese and olive oil, but you can make your own version with any fresh herbs, garlic and olive oil. The important thing to remember is that the herbs must be absolutely fresh, and used in quantity. Depending which herbs are available, take handfuls each of basil and parsley, coriander and chervil, or rosemary and sage, and chop finely. Add 2 chopped cloves garlic and ½ chopped dried chilli. Season, and cover generously with good olive oil until needed. Pesto can be kept for weeks in the fridge so long as it is sealed from the air by a covering of olive oil.

## PASTA WITH HERB PESTO

Cook spaghetti in plenty of boiling salted water until al dente. Drain and toss with herb pesto, 50g/2oz grated Parmesan and more olive oil.

## HERB FRITTATA

A frittata is an Italian omelette cooked in olive oil. Mix 6 fresh eggs with a handful of freshly-picked chopped herbs such as parsley, chervil and basil, then season. Heat a pan with olive oil, pour in the egg mixture and cook gently on a low heat. When the frittata is cooked on the bottom, but still runny on top, remove the pan from the heat and sprinkle on 2 tbspns grated Parmesan cheese. Grill for 1 minute or until just brown — do not overcook — and serve at room temperature.

## PIZZA BIANCA WITH ROSEMARY

To make the pizza dough, first stir 45g/1½oz fresh yeast into 300ml/½ pint warm water with salt and 1 tbspn olive oil and leave to dissolve for about 10 minutes. Pour 600g/1¼lb plain flour onto a work surface and make a well in the centre. Add the yeast, drop by drop, into the well, whilst mixing in the flour with your hands. Knead the dough into a ball and leave to rise in a warm place for 1 hour in a covered bowl. When risen, press the dough gently with your hand into 10 thin rounds, each about 6mm/¼in thick. Sprinkle on some freshly picked rosemary, salt and a drizzle of olive oil. Bake in a hot oven for 8-15 minutes until beginning to brown around the edges.

# HERB OILS

This setting has an unaffected charm and simplicity, with its crisp blue and white linen cloth and continuing blue and white theme of individual chairs and polka-dotted china, jugs and bowls of fresh garden pickings.

Many varieties of basil grow well in Tuscany, where their fresh leaves are used liberally for pesto, in sauces and with tomatoes and other summer vegetables. In sunny climates, the small-leaved Greek basil makes a fragrant edging plant to border part of a herb garden. Whether growing basil in the garden or in pots in a sunny sheltered place, always pinch out the flowers when they appear and this judicious pruning will encourage the plant to bush and more leaves to grow. Midsummer, when it is in plentiful supply, is the time to pick basil and retain its matchless flavour in oils and sauces for the winter. Nothing is more reminiscent of warm summer days than a spoonful of pesto in a winter soup, or a salad dressing made with basil-flavoured oil. Pick all the leaves from the stalks of a large plant. Wash and dry well. Put in a preserving jar, completely cover with a good virgin olive oil, add some black peppercorns and seal the jar.

Tuscan olive oil is a basic ingredient in all Tricia Guild's cooking. Light and golden, heavy and green, fruity or scented, the earthy flavour of rich oil should change from cooking to salads. Virgin olive oil, dark and green from the first cold pressing, is best for salads, whilst a lighter, golden one can be used for cooking.

# SALADS

Climbing up stakes, sweet peas and fresh peas flower amidst the borage, thyme and sage in the blue section of Tricia Guild's kitchen garden, with its rough wooden dividers and box border. Beyond, in the red section, nasturtiums, tomatoes staked in rows, strawberries, radishes and berries flourish together. This produce is picked throughout the year fresh for the table. After a winter diet of root vegetables, the first spring greens of lettuce, arugula (rocket) and other salad leaves are not only a delicious cleanser but also an important source of vitamins and minerals. If you have room, grow as many varieties of salad leaf as possible — oak leaf, butterhead and romaine lettuces, lollo rosso, radicchio and rocket amongst them. Use straight from the garden and toss with a handful of mixed herbs and their flowers and a dressing made from good olive oil, a few drops of balsamic vinegar, salt and pepper. Grated and blanched zucchini with toasted pine nuts and a dash of olive oil makes a colourful alternative, arranged in a radicchio leaf and garnished with coriander or chervil.

# VEGETABLES

Summer vegetables, sliced and marinated in olive oil with herbs and garlic, then grilled, are a favourite luncheon dish in Tricia Guild's household. Glossy purple aubergines (sliced and then soaked in salted water to remove any bitterness), peppers of every hue, zucchini, fennel, potatoes and even flat mushrooms are marinated, then grilled on a griddle pan or simply placed under a hot grill or on a barbecue. Olive oil and garlic are the basic marinade for any grilled vegetable, but each has a particular herb which marries well with its flavour — mint with zucchini, basil with aubergine, chervil and parsley with potato.

Little round zucchini or squash are common in Mediterranean countries, but more difficult to find elsewhere, unless you grow your own. Trim, wash and bake them in the oven with olive oil, thyme, salt and pepper for about 20 minutes, then leave to stand a few minutes before serving.

### ZUCCHINI AND MINT RISOTTO

Heat about 1l/1¾ pints good chicken or vegetable stock. In another pan, sauté 1 finely chopped medium onion in oil. Add 350g/12oz Arborio rice and stir into the oil until slightly transparent. Add a ladleful of hot stock and stir until absorbed. Continue the process, adding stock and stirring until absorbed for 25-30 minutes or until the rice is cooked but still slightly al dente. After 20 minutes, add 2 diced and blanched zucchini and about 25g/1oz finely chopped fresh mint. Once the rice is cooked, add a little butter (if desired) and 2 tbspns grated Parmesan cheese. Season to taste and serve at once. Serves 4.

# TOMATOES

Tomatoes are a staple of Italian cooking, each region boasting a range of varieties. In the basket is a selection of those grown in Tricia Guild's garden: from left to right, pointed plum tomatoes which grow full of flesh with barely any cavity or core and little juice, therefore ideal for bottling; small fruited plum tomatoes which make wonderful sauces and purées and can be dried for use later in the year; bright red beefsteak tomatoes, excellent sliced and served simply with mozzarella cheese and basil leaves, or skinned and coarsely chopped into flavoursome sauces; tiny red cherry tomatoes for salads.

### HOME-DRIED TOMATOES

Halve some tomatoes, preferably a mixture of plum and round varieties. Remove most of the seeds, sprinkle with salt, put on a baking tray cut side up and cook in a very low oven for 12 hours or overnight. When done they will wrinkle up and become much darker in colour. Pack into jars and cover with olive oil. Keep in a cool place.

### TOMATO AND ZUCCHINI PIZZA

Make the pizza dough and leave to rise (see *Pizza Bianca with Rosemary* page 144). Sauté 1 chopped clove garlic in oil, add 12 Moulied or skinned and chopped ripe plum tomatoes and simmer for 15 minutes. Press out enough dough for the pizza base (the rest can be frozen), cover with a layer of tomato sauce and bake in a very hot oven for 15 minutes. Remove and add layers of dried tomato halves, blanched and sliced zucchini and shaved Parmesan cheese. Drizzle with oil and bake for 5-10 minutes. Top with sprigs of fresh basil and serve.

The ubiquitous tomato sauce, found all over the world on pasta and pizzas, is best freshly made and can be used as an accompaniment to gnocchi or gnudi (vegetable dumplings bound with flour and egg). A raw tomato sauce livened up with rocket and toasted almonds can be used to dress pasta. Rocket, or arugula, is simple to grow, as its name suggests. It can be sown successively throughout the year for a constant supply and will even continue to flourish in winter if protected from frost. Its sharp, peppery taste is particularly welcome in the winter months when fresh salad leaves are hard to find.

### SPAGHETTI WITH RAW TOMATO AND ROCKET

Cook the spaghetti in plenty of salted boiling water. Meanwhile sauté 1 chopped clove garlic in oil, then add 8 roughly chopped plum tomatoes. Allow to heat through without cooking and add 1 tbspn toasted chopped almonds and a large handful chopped fresh rocket leaves. Toss with the drained spaghetti and serve at once.

### SPINACH GNUDI

Chop half a small onion and sauté in oil until golden. Add 635g/1¼lb cooked, finely-chopped spinach, and sauté for 5 minutes with a sprinkling of salt. Cool slightly then, in a large bowl, mix thoroughly with 250g/10oz ricotta cheese and 100g/4oz plain flour. Add 3 egg yolks, a pinch of nutmeg and 150g/6oz freshly grated pecorino or Parmesan cheese. Season to taste, then work together well and chill. Shape into round balls and cook, a few at a time, in a large pan of salted boiling water for 3-4 minutes. Serve with fresh tomato sauce and basil. Serves 6.

# PASTA

Pasta is the ultimate convenience food. There are countless different shapes — one manufacturer's catalogue lists 52 varieties — and many well-known shapes are called by different names in different parts of Italy. The major difference is between dried pasta made from durum wheat with water and fresh pasta, which contains egg. Sauces can be made from virtually any ingredient, but the northern, meat and dairy-based sauces generally go better with fresh pasta, whilst dried pasta suits the stronger southern, garlic and vegetable-based mixtures. All pasta should be cooked in a large saucepan in masses of salted boiling water, uncovered, and stirred frequently. Cooking times vary depending on the shape and the make, but in general dried pasta takes 8-15 minutes, whilst fresh egg pasta takes only a few minutes. A few drops of olive oil added to the water will help to keep the strands separate. Above, from left to right, these fresh samples from a Tuscan market are gnocchi, tagliatelle, fettucine, spaghetti and linguine, interlaced with sprigs of thyme.

## LINGUINE WITH BROCCOLI, OLIVES AND CAPERS

Cook 500g/1lb broccoli florets until tender but still slightly crisp and drain. Cook the linguine in plenty of salted boiling water. Meanwhile, sauté 1 chopped onion until soft and turning colour. Add the broccoli with 75g/3oz stoned black olives and 2 tbspns drained capers. Heat, season and toss with the drained linguine. Garnish with flat-leaved parsley and freshly-grated Parmesan or pecorino cheese. Serve in bowls or on plates which complement the colours of the sauce, such as the Designers Guild hand-painted tableware shown on these pages.

## SPAGHETTI ALLA PUTTANESCA

Sauté 2 chopped cloves of garlic and 1 chopped onion until starting to change colour. Add 1l/1¾ pints preserved tomatoes or 1kg/2¼lb peeled and chopped fresh tomatoes. Cook for 10 minutes, then add 8 chopped anchovies, 1 tbspn capers and 2 tbspns stoned black olives. Cover and cook for about 30 minutes on a low heat. Meanwhile, cook the pasta in plenty of boiling salted water. Drain and toss with the sauce.

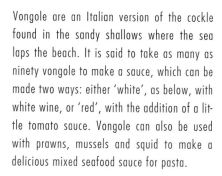

Vongole are an Italian version of the cockle found in the sandy shallows where the sea laps the beach. It is said to take as many as ninety vongole to make a sauce, which can be made two ways: either 'white', as below, with white wine, or 'red', with the addition of a little tomato sauce. Vongole can also be used with prawns, mussels and squid to make a delicious mixed seafood sauce for pasta.

## SPAGHETTI ALLE VONGOLE

Clean 1kg/2¼lb vongole as you would mussels. Cook the spaghetti in plenty of salted boiling water. Meanwhile, sauté 1 chopped onion, 2 cloves garlic and 1 chilli pepper, add the vongole, salt, pepper and ½ glass white wine. Cover and cook quickly for a few minutes. When all the shells are open, pour over the drained spaghetti and toss with a handful of chopped parsley.

## TAGLIATELLE WITH CELERY AND PANCETTA

Chop 1 head of celery into fine slices and roughly chop 1 onion, 4 slices pancetta (or smoked streaky bacon) and 1 dried chilli. Sauté the pancetta, then remove from the pan. Sauté the onion in oil, then add pancetta, celery, chilli, ½ tspn fennel seeds and ½ glass white wine. Continue to cook until the celery is tender but still slightly crunchy. Cook the tagliatelle in plenty of salted boiling water. Drain and toss with the sauce. Serve with 50g/2oz grated Parmesan cheese, garnished with celery leaves and chervil.

# FISH

Fish caught in local waters, however unfamiliar, are generally more rewarding than those that have spent days on ice travelling to your local fish shop. More so than with any other kind of ingredient, it is vital that fish is fresh. Their eyes should be bright, the flesh firm and cool. If freshly caught, fish need very little cooking or additional flavouring. Simple baking with herbs will bring out their true flavour.

## BAKED SEA BASS

Clean a large fish and stuff it with sprigs of fresh rosemary, then season and put in a roasting tin with more rosemary, lemon slices and olive oil. Cover the tin with foil and bake for 20 minutes (depending on size). Then remove the foil and continue baking for 5-10 minutes. Remove the fish to a serving dish, pour over the juices and keep warm. Serve with a sauce made from 100ml/4fl oz olive oil, the juice of 1 lemon, and 2 tbspns chopped parsley.

## BAKED SEA BREAM WITH OLIVES AND TOMATOES

Bream is a firm, fleshy fish with a distinctive flavour, so it can take this strong Mediterranean sauce, which would also suit any oily fish from northern waters. Clean the fish, then stuff with sprigs of fresh rosemary, thyme and oregano and season. Chop 8 plum tomatoes into large chunks and add about 75g/3oz stoned olives, 2 crushed garlic cloves and more herbs. Put this mixture around the fish and pour over olive oil and ½ glass white wine. Cover with foil and bake. Small fish will take 15-20 minutes, larger fish closer to 30 minutes. They are done when the flesh parts easily from the backbone.

# MUSHROOMS

The porcino mushroom, *Boletus edulis*, otherwise known in France as cep, in England as Penny Bun, is one of Italy's greatest exports, being available dried throughout the world. If using dried porcini clean them well to remove the grit, then soak in warm water or a mixture of olive oil and water to bring firmness back to the flesh. Squeeze well to remove moisture before using; the liquid can be strained and added to a sauce.

### GRILLED PORCINI

The most delicious of wild mushrooms when freshly picked. Wipe the mushrooms clean, remove the stalks and arrange 4 slivers of garlic on top of each mushroom cap and 4 underneath. Drizzle olive oil over them and grill. Garnish with chopped flat-leaved parsley or mint.

### MUSHROOM RISOTTO

For the basic risotto recipe, see *Zucchini and Mint Risotto* (page 150). Roughly cut or tear 300g/10oz mixed wild mushrooms such as porcini, chanterelles and oyster mushrooms. Sauté with garlic, salt and pepper, then add to the basic risotto 5 minutes before the end of cooking. Serve with freshly-grated Parmesan cheese. This recipe can also be made with dried porcini, using the liquid that the porcini were soaked in as part of the stock. However, fresh mushrooms will definitely give a more delicate flavour.

### PORCINI AND FENNEL SALAD

Slice the tops and stalks of fresh porcini. Sauté 1 clove crushed garlic in a pan, add the porcini and cook briskly for 5-7 minutes. When cooked, remove from the heat and add a little more oil and a dash of balsamic vinegar. Serve on a bed of sliced fennel and garnish with chopped chervil.

### WILD MUSHROOM SALAD

Sauté mixed wild mushrooms with garlic and serve on a bed of salad leaves. Garnish with mixed herbs such as oregano, parsley, chervil and mint.

### OVOLI, FENNEL AND PARMESAN SALAD

Ovoli (*Amanita caesarea*) or Caesar's mushroom, are a rarity in Italy. If you are lucky enough to come across this delicious variety, prepare simply in a salad to appreciate the delicate flavour. Slice them finely and serve raw with sliced fennel, shavings of Parmesan cheese, salt and pepper and a drizzle of the best olive oil.

# CURED MEATS

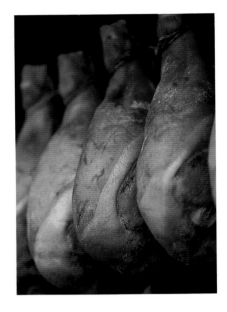

Everything about country life is the antithesis of urban living, and the purchase and enjoyment of food is no exception. How much more enjoyable to wander around your local open-air market, with its mixture of stalls selling everything from furnishing materials to garden tools, and all manner of locally grown and produced foods displayed on rough wooden boards or wrapped in their own leaves.

Regional specialities such as cured and smoked meats and handmade cheeses, their recipes hundreds of years in the refining, long time in the making, are all the better savoured at leisure with some fresh bread, a salad and a glass of wine. Meals such as these need no planning, they just come together as the marriage of flavours is found through pleasurable trial and error.

The Italians are past masters at putting together combinations of man-made foods and natural produce – Parma ham with melon or, better still, with sun-ripened, midsummer, green and purple figs; pecorino or Parmesan cheese with pears; mozzarella with tomato, the sweet, fresh ripeness of one complementing the maturity or pungent taste of the other.

Two or three ingredients are put together on a plate which shows off their textures and colours, garnished with a few leaves from the garden or a newly-picked string of olives or tomatoes. There are times when a meal of complete simplicity will prove more memorable than the best restaurant meal.

# FRUIT & CHEESE

The best Parmesan, parmigiano-reggiano, gets its name from the precise area where it is legally entitled to be produced in the provinces of Parma and Reggio Emilia, in the Emilia-Romagna region. Its uses are many and varied: grated on pasta, combined with olive oil and pine nuts to make pesto, cooked in a variety of dishes. Fresh, its flavour is perhaps best appreciated when thinly shaved to accompany fruit, a salad of young leaves or early summer vegetables such as asparagus.

Pecorino, a cheese made from ewe's milk, is made in Sicily and Sardinia, as well as in Rome and Tuscany. Abroad, the best known is Roman pecorino, a hard, oily cheese which is used mainly for grating over pasta as a stronger alternative to Parmesan. From Sicily comes a version of pecorino which is often flavoured with saffron or studded with peppercorns. But the most sought-after is Tuscan pecorino, made in early spring when the young grass is at its greenest, imparting its fresh flavour to the crumbly round cheeses. Pecorino can be eaten when first made or at various stages of maturity; it is the perfect complement to the sweet crisp taste of a ripe pear.

Bunches of green and black grapes, plucked straight from vine to table, finish off a meal with caprino, a tiny goat's cheese, and delicate ricotta, also made from ewe's or buffalo milk and used in many Italian desserts and as a filling for ravioli and other pasta.

# FLOWERS

By using flowers imaginatively the mood of a room can completely change, from urban sophistication to relaxed country charm. Sometimes only one or two individual flowers or flower heads will be enough to brighten a table setting — a sprig of blossom on a plate, flower heads garnishing a dish or tossed into a salad, some herbs upon each plate. The success of Tricia Guild's arrangements is their lack of formality and apparently random groupings, often concentrating on shades of one colour, such as heads of delphinium ranging from palest blue to deep purple. Once you start to grow flowers you appreciate their individual blooms in the garden and are more careful about which to cut. Containers don't have to be grand — a tin pot, a bucket or an earthenware jug will do — but think of the flowers in their setting. Their colours must work with the fabric and ceramics around them, the vibrant contrasts creating a feeling of exhilaration and joyfulness. Bowls of fresh fruit or vegetables from the garden can become part of the table setting if arranged to complement it in coloured groupings.

# DESSERTS

Purpling berries raised up from a basketweave background, a grape leaf on feathery ferns raised above the surface, these precious majolica plates are thrown into relief by the plain white background on which they sit. With such fine tableware, only the best white-upon-white embroidered napkins and cloth will do, but to defuse the formality a single scented leaf and a zinnia are set in an old inkwell. This strikes a contrast with the finest old linen, crystal and amber-handled silver cutlery. The colours change again when sweet dessert wine is poured into the glasses to impart its ambered sweetness to a dish of fresh berries — raspberries, strawberries, red and black currants, bought in punnets in the market, brought home and turned into ice cream and crimson coulis.

### RASPBERRY ICE CREAM

Bring 400ml/14fl oz milk to the boil. Whisk 5 large egg yolks and 50g/2oz sugar together until white. Whisk the boiling milk into the yolk mixture, pour back into the pan and stir well over low heat, taking care not to boil, until beginning to thicken. Pour into a bowl over ice to cool very fast, adding 350g/12oz raspberry purée. When cold, churn in an ice cream machine. As an alternative, mix 750ml/1¼ pints natural yoghurt with 350ml/12fl oz sweetened raspberry purée and then churn. Serves 6.

### RED BERRY COULIS

Use either 300g/10oz raspberries or a mixture of different red berries. Blend the berries with the juice of half a lemon and sugar to taste. Serve over red fruit ice cream. Garnish with mint.

In late summer, an abundance of fruit appears on the trees and subsequently in the markets. This area of Tuscany produces a glut of peaches, pears, apricots and figs. All these fruits can be enjoyed fresh in many ways, or preserved to add their golden summer flavour to winter meals. To capture the sweet essence of peaches, slice thinly, sprinkle with sugar, a little lemon juice and perhaps some dessert wine and chill. Serve on painted plates to show off their rich colours and top with home-made ice cream and a sprig of mint.

To release the honeyed flavour of fresh apricots, cut in half and stone, then cook with a little sugar and a vanilla pod in just enough water to cover. Remove when just soft and reduce the syrup before pouring over. Or make this wonderful apricot tart, best served freshly baked and still warm. Rich in vitamins and minerals, apricots can be dried in the late summer sun and stored for use in winter compotes and soufflés.

### PEACH ICE CREAM

Make the basic ice cream recipe (see *Raspberry Ice Cream* page 175), adding 350ml/12fl oz peach purée made from fresh skinned peaches and juice of half a lemon as the mixture cools. Arrange a plate with sliced peaches that have been soaked in a little lemon juice and sugar, putting the ice cream in the centre.

### APRICOT TART

For the shortcrust pastry, sift 225g/8oz plain flour into a bowl and cut in 150g/5oz butter in pieces. Add 1 tbspn icing or caster sugar and rub in the mixture. Make a well in the centre, add 1 egg yolk mixed with 1 tablespoon water and mix with a fork. Knead on a wooden board for a minute and then chill for 30 minutes before rolling out and lining a lightly greased flan dish.

For the filling, arrange approx 1 kg/2¼lb stoned, halved apricots in circles in the lined dish. Mix 2 egg yolks with 150ml/¼ pint single cream, 150ml/¼ pint milk and 1 tbspn sugar and pour over the apricots. Sprinkle with pine nuts and bake in a medium oven for 40 minutes.

One can almost feel the warmth of the sun on this rustic table laden with produce. Fruits that have been allowed to ripen on the plant really develop their full flavours and taste of the ground in which they grew. Served in an individual way, freshly upon a plate to be enjoyed, these small seasonal pleasures bring a sense of well-being to everyday life.

The pure whiteness of homemade panna cotta (literally 'cooked cream') is thrown into relief against the trompe l'oeil mixture of berries on the raised majolica plate, itself set off by the crisply folded red-striped linen cloth. Nothing can beat the mouthwatering contrast between the sharp fruity taste of the berries and the smooth creamy texture of this summer pudding.

### PANNA COTTA WITH BERRIES

Dissolve 2¾ leaves of gold leaf gelatine in 225ml/8fl oz cold milk. Bring 750ml/1¼ pints double cream with 50g/2oz sugar and a vanilla pod to the boil, then simmer for 2 minutes. Add the gelatine and milk and stir in. Pour into moulds, allow to cool completely, then put into the fridge to set for a minimum of 2 hours.

Meanwhile, put the mixed berries in a bowl and sprinkle on a little sugar and white wine. Leave to soak for about an hour. To serve, arrange around the panna cotta and pour over a little fruit coulis (see page 175).

From April to October fresh berries cluster on bushes and plants in the garden — red, white and black currants, strawberries large and small, raspberries. In September the blackberries arrive in the hedgerows, small and spicy at this age, to be set in a spiralling pattern upon a layer of jam in a fruit tart. The rich reds of the fruits are sharpened by the addition of bright green mint leaves and the complementary green of the strawberry leaves on a folded red and white napkin.

### BERRY TART

For the shortcrust pastry, sift 225g/8oz plain flour into a bowl and cut in 150g/5oz butter in pieces. Add 1 tbspn icing or caster sugar and rub in the mixture. Make a well in the centre, add 1 egg yolk mixed with 1 tablespoon water and mix with a fork. Knead on a wooden board for a minute and then chill for 30 minutes.

Roll out the chilled dough and line a tart tin, then bake blind for 15 minutes, take out and allow to cool. When cold, spread a thin layer of red berry jam over the base. Arrange the berries in a pattern and garnish with a sprig of mint or strawberry leaves. Serve with a fruit coulis and mascarpone or thick creamy yoghurt.

As the season advances and late summer fruits such as plums and damsons introduce a purple bloom to the table, the settings are similarly darkened with blues, ochres and dark greens, Michaelmas daisies and chrysanthemums. Patterned Indian cloths and shaped, hand-painted dishes and bowls bring more intense colours to the table.

## PLUM TART

For the shortcrust pastry, sift 225g/8oz plain flour into a bowl and cut in 150g/5oz butter in pieces. Add 1 tbspn icing or caster sugar and rub in the mixture. Make a well in the centre, add 1 egg yolk mixed with 1 tablespoon water and mix with a fork. Knead on a wooden board for a minute and then chill for 30 minutes.

Roll out the chilled dough into a thin circle and put onto an ovenproof plate. Spread with a layer of plum jam. Take 1kg/2¼lb Switzen plums, cut in halves and make 2 slits at the top of each to make a petal shape. Arrange the plums on the base, starting at the outer edge, with each layer slightly overlapping the next. Sprinkle with caster sugar and bake for 30-40 minutes in a medium oven. Serve warm.

A winter compote, made from the last of the season's peaches, pears, plums and figs, is a welcome reminder of summer. When the frosts have come and there is no more warm sun to ripen the fruits on the trees, a compote can be made from dried fruits softened by cooking in water with a little fruit juice or wine. Served either with yoghurt for a healthy winter breakfast, or with mascarpone or crème fraîche at the end of a meal, the taste of the soft fruits can be enhanced by sweet dessert wine and given a contrasting nutty texture with little homemade biscuits such as these cantucci or ricciarelli.

### CANTUCCI

Preheat the oven to 190°C/375°F/Gas 5. Toast some blanched almonds and roughly chop them with 150g/5oz pine nuts. Sift 500g/1lb flour onto a pastry board and make a well in the centre. Pour in 4 beaten eggs with some baking powder and a pinch of salt. Work this to a smooth consistency with your hands, then mix in the nuts. Roll pieces of dough into long fingers and bake for 15 minutes. Remove and slice on the diagonal, then bake for another 25 minutes.

### RICCIARELLI

Crush 350g/12oz almonds with a mortar and mix with 250g/9oz caster sugar. Put in a large bowl and fold in 2 whisked egg whites, adding 180g/6oz icing sugar and 1 tbspn grated orange peel, until it makes a smooth paste. Form into diamond-shaped lozenges and hust heavily with icing sugar. Place on a sheet of rice paper and leave for 12 hours, then bake in a very low oven for about 15 minutes. Cool and dust with more icing sugar.

# DESIGNERS GUILD STOCKISTS

Designers Guild fabric, wallpaper, sofas, chairs and ottomans are available from
Designers Guild Stores
267 and 277 Kings Road
London SW3 5EN.
Tel: 071-351 5775 and from selected retailers in the United Kingdom and Eire including:

**AVON**
Michael Bracey Interiors
30 The Mall, Clifton
Bristol BS8 4DS
Tel: 0272 734664

**BERKSHIRE**
Christine Scott Interiors
50 Northbrook Street
Newbury RG13 1DT
Tel: 0635 551372

**BUCKINGHAMSHIRE**
Morgan Gilder Furnishings
83 High Street
Stony Stratford
Milton Keynes MK11 1AT
Tel: 0908 568674

**CAMBRIDGESHIRE**
At Home
44 Newnham Road
Cambridge CB3 9EY
Tel: 0223 321283

**CHANNEL ISLANDS**
The Designers Choice
21 Seale Street
St Helier
Jersey JE2 3QG
Tel: 0534 24678

J&J Interior Design Consultants
Glategny Chambers
Glategny Esplanade
St Peter Port
Guernsey GY1 2LP
Tel: 0481 710388

**CHESHIRE**
Designers
15 London Road
Alderley Edge SK9 7UT
Tel: 0625 586851

**CORNWALL**
Casa Fina Interiors
29 River Street
Truro TR1 2SJ
Tel: 0872 70818

**DERBYSHIRE**
Classic Interiors
6a High Street
Buxton SK17 6EU
Tel: 0298 72063

Interior Design
Matlock Street
Bakewell DE45 1EE
Tel: 0629 813263

**DEVON**
G&H Interiors
1 The Old Pannier Market
High Street
Honiton EX 14 8LS
Tel: 0404 42063

**DORSET**
Country Seats
The Square
Beaminster DT8 3AS
Tel: 0308 863545

Individual Interior Design
58-60 Poole Road
Westbourne
Bournemouth BH4 9DZ
Tel: 0202 763256

County Interiors
2 East Borough
Wimborne BH21 1PF
Tel: 0202 880959

**EIRE**
Geraldine Hudson Interiors
2 Herbert Lane
Dublin 2
Tel: 010 353 16600325

**ESSEX**
Clement Joscelyne Ltd
9-11 High Street
Brentwood CM14 4RG
Tel: 0277 225420

Gillian Anne Designs
30-32 High Road
Buckhurst Hill IG9 5HP
Tel: 081-504 4875/7925

**GLOUCESTERSHIRE**
Jon Edgson Designs & Decoration
38 Dyer Street
Cirencester GL7 2PF
Tel: 0285 640886

**GREATER MANCHESTER**
Homes Unlimited
2 Warburton Street
Didsbury Village
Manchester M20 0RA
Tel: 061 434 6278

**HAMPSHIRE**
Pat Staples Interiors
Symes Corner
1 Houchin Street
Bishops Waltham SO3 1AR
Tel: 0489 892626

**HEREFORD & WORCESTERSHIRE**
John Nash Antiques and Interiors
Tudor House
17c High Street
Ledbury HR8 1DS
Tel: 0531 635714

**HERTFORDSHIRE**
Clement Joscelyne Ltd
Market Square
Bishop's Stortford CM23 3XA
Tel: 0279 506731

Codicote House Interiors
106 High Street
Codicote
Hitchin SG4 8XE
Tel: 0438 820294

**KENT**
John Thornton Interiors
43 St Peter's Street
Canterbury CT1 2BG
Tel: 0227 785284

Kent House Sofas
206 Kent House Road
Beckenham BR3 1JN
Tel: 081-778 7782

Kotiki Interiors
22-24 Grove Hill Road
Tunbridge Wells TN1 1RZ
Tel: 0892 521369

Wallpaper World
5 Simpsons Road
Bromley BR2 9AP
Tel: 081-460 9089

**LANCASHIRE**
Campion
24 High Street
Uppermill
Saddleworth
Nr Oldham OL3 6HX
Tel: 0457 876341

Grahams Interiors
402/4 Bolton Road West
Holcombe Brook
Ramsbottom BL0 9RY
Tel: 0204 884911

**LEICESTERSHIRE**
Harlequin Interiors
11 Loseby Lane
Leicester LE1 5DR
Tel: 0533 620994

**LINCOLNSHIRE**
Pilgrim Decor
35 Wide Bargate
Boston PE21 6SR
Tel: 0205 363917

**LONDON**
Baer & Ingram Wallpapers
273 Wandsworth Bridge Road
London SW6 2TX
Tel: 071-736 6111

Harrods
87/135 Brompton Road
Knightsbridge
London SW1X 7XL
Tel: 071-730 1234

Heal & Son
196 Tottenham Court Road
London W1P 9LD
Tel: 071-636 1666

Interiors Of Chiswick
454-458 Chiswick High Road
London W4 5TT
Tel: 081-994 0073

Liberty
Regent Street
London W1 6AH
Tel: 071-734 1234

**MERSEYSIDE**
Judi James Interiors
229 Rose Lane
Allerton
Liverpool L18 5HJ
Tel: 051 724 2956

**MIDDLESEX**
Gallenti
37-39 High Street
Pinner HA5 5PJ
Tel: 081-868 2013

**NORFOLK**
Clement Joscelyne Ltd
The Granary 5 Bedford Street
Norwich NR2 1AL
Tel: 0603 623220

**NORTHANTS**
Classix
The Old Trinity Church
247 Wellingborough Road
Northampton NN1 4EH
Tel: 0604 232322

**NORTHERN IRELAND**
Fultons Fine Furnishings
55-63 Queen Street
Lurgan BT66 8BN
Tel: 0762 325768

**NOTTINGHAMSHIRE**
Nash Interiors
17-19 Carlton Street
Nottingham NG1 1NL
Tel: 0602 413891

**OXON**
Pipkins Interiors
68 Church Way
Iffley
Oxford OX4 4EF
Tel: 0865 777147

**SCOTLAND**
Cairns Interiors
111-113 High Street
Old Aberdeen AB2 3EN
Tel: 0224 487490

Decor (Aberdeen) Ltd
157 Skene Street
Aberdeen AB1 1QL
Tel: 0224 646533

Designworks
38 Gibson Street
Glasgow G12 8NX
Tel: 041 339 9520

Mary Maxwell Designs
63 Dublin Street
Edinburgh EH3 6NS
Tel: 031 557 2173

Number Thirty-Five
35 Bridge Street
Dollar
Clacknammanshire FK14 7EZ
Tel: 0259 743339

**SOMERSET**
Paul Carter Interiors
The Studio
Elm House
6 Chip Lane
Taunton TA1 1BZ
Tel: 0823 330404

**STAFFORDSHIRE**
The William Morris Shop
313 Hartshill Road, Hartshill
Stoke-on-Trent ST4 7NR
Tel: 0782 619772

**SUFFOLK**
Clement Joscelyne Ltd
16 Langton Place
Bury St Edmunds IP33 1NE
Tel: 0284 753 824

Edwards of Hadleigh
53 High Street
Hadleigh IP7 5AB
Tel: 0473 827271

**SURREY**
Katherine Letts Interiors
127 High Street
Godalming GU7 1AF
Tel: 0483 860106

Sage Antiques & Interiors
The Green Cottage
High Street
Ripley GU23 6BB
Tel: 0483 224396

Sue Ralston Designs
8 Station Approach
Kew Gardens
Richmond TW9 3QB
Tel: 081-940 7756

SUSSEX
Patricia's of Findon
170 Kings Parade
Findon Road
Findon Valley
West Sussex BN14 0EL
Tel: 0903 692666

Pine & Design Interiors
Haywards Heath Road
Balcombe RH17 2PE
Tel: 0444 811700

Suttons Furnishings
56 Church Road
Hove BN3 2BD
Tel: 0273 723728

The Easy Chair Company
30 Lyndhurst Road
Worthing BN11 2DF
Tel: 0903 201081

TYNE & WEAR
Abercrombies
142 Manor House Road
Jesmond
Newcastle Upon Tyne NE2 2NA
Tel: 091 281 7182

Studio Interiors Ltd
4 Old George Yard
Cloth Market
Newcastle Upon Tyne NE1 1EZ
Tel: 091 261 4575

WALES
Country Interiors
Goat Street
Haverfordwest
Dyfed SA61 1PX
Tel: 0437 768217

WARWICKSHIRE
Arnold & Bainbridge
30 Smith Street
Warwick CV34 4HS
Tel: 0926 490020

WEST MIDLANDS
Bennett & Bowman Interiors Ltd
4 Beeches Walk
Sutton Coldfield B73 6NN
Tel: 021 354 9371

John Charles Interiors
349 Hagley Road
Edgbaston
Birmingham B17 8DN
Tel: 021 4203977

John Hewins Interiors
1663 High Street
Knowle
Solihull B93 0LL
Tel: 0564 772544

J.W. Treadwell
342-344 Stratford Road
Shirley
Solihull BG0 3DW
Tel: 021 745 3241

YORKSHIRE
'Andrena's' Soft Furnishings &
Design
18 Leeds Road
Ilkley LS29 8DJ
Tel: 0943 607185

Cedar House Interiors
7 The Village, Haxby
York YO3 3HS
Tel: 0904 764894

Designer Drapes
217 Bingley Road
Saltaire BD18 4ON
Tel: 0274 593211

Philip Walton
162 Main Street
Addingham
Nr Ilkley LS29 0NA
Tel: 0943 831258

Sue Rugg
Soft Furnishing Design Specialist
11 Eastgate
Bramhope
Leeds LS16 9AT
Tel: 0532 842960

Plaskitt & Plaskitt
8A Walmgate
York YO1 2TJ
Tel: 0904 624670
       0532 432224

Designers Guild products are
available worldwide through
selected representatives including
the following:

AUSTRALIA
Wardlaw Pty Ltd
230-232 Auburn Road
Hawthorn
3122 Melbourne
Victoria
Tel: 03 819 4233

Wardlaw Pty Ltd
100 Harris Street
Pyrmont 2009, N.S.W.
Tel: 02 660 6266

Wardlaw Pty Ltd
36 Vernon Terrace
Newstead 4006
Queensland
Tel: 07 257 1642

Wardlaw Pty Ltd
2A Close Street
Rose Park 5067, S.A.
Tel: 08 332 2111

Wardlaw Pty Ltd
263A Stirling Highway
Claremont 6010, W.A.
Tel: 09 383 4833

AUSTRIA
Victoria Schoeller-Szuts
Borsegasse 9/10
A-1010 Vienna
Tel: 01 535 3075

BELGIUM & LUXEMBOURG
Carl sprl
Avenue de l'Hippodrome 5
B-1050 Brussels
Tel: 02 640 8570

CYPRUS
L.I. Christofides Ltd
9 Loukis Akritas Avenue
PO Box B10 Nicosia
Tel: 02 462 939

DENMARK
Designers Guild Denmark
Bukkeballevej 24
2960 Rungsted Kyst
Tel: 042 864 480

FRANCE
Designers Guild Chez Etamine
2 Rue de Furstenberg
75006 PARIS
Tel: 43 25 49 83

FINLAND
Interfurn OY AB
Marjaniemenranta 31
SF-00930 Helsingfors
Tel: 080 7001 7650

GERMANY
Designers Guild Einrichtungs GmbH
Sendlinger Tor Platz 6
80336 Munich
Tel: 089 2311620

GREECE
Persefone N Diamandas & CO EE
14 Filikis Eterias Square
GR-106 73 Athens
Tel: 01 360 9324

HONG KONG
Gallaria Furnishings Int. Ltd
LG3 Cavendish Centre
23 Yip Hing Street
Wong Chuk Hang
Tel: 552 8300

ICELAND
Best Design
Skol. 12
Reykjavik
Tel: 04 112 920

ISRAEL
Sezam Ltd
255 Dizengoff Street
Shop 406
63117 Tel-Aviv
Tel: 03 354 6352

ITALY
Blue Home Distribution spa
via Tevere 24
50019 Loc. Osmannoro
Sesto Fiorentino (FL)
Tel: 055 311 795

JAPAN
Fujie Textile Co Ltd
No 7-12 4-Chome
Sendagaya
Shibuyaku
Tokyo 151
Tel: 03 3405 1312

KUWAIT
Al Sedrah
M/S Abdulla Alomar Alyagout
PO Box 206
13003 Safat
Tel: 264 9466

MEXICO
Artell SA de CV
Altavista no. 120
Col San Angel Inn
Mexico 01000 DF
Tel: 05 272 2861

NETHERLANDS
Wilhelmine van Aerssen
Roemer Visscherstraat 48
1054 EZ Amsterdam
Tel: 020 6836 854

NEW ZEALAND
Mokum Textiles Ltd
11 Cheshire Street
Parnell, Auckland 1
Tel: 09 379 3041

NORWAY
Design Works
Kirkeveien 56
0368 Oslo
Tel: 022 46 56 41

PORTUGAL
Pedroso E Osorio
Rua Fernao Lopes 409-2
4100 Oporto
Tel: 02 617 1497

SAUDI ARABIA
Ahmed G Alesayi
PO Box 5651
Jeddah 21432
Tel: 02 669 0071

SINGAPORE
Linea Tre
402 Orchard Road
04-02/05 Delphi Orchard
Singapore 0923
Tel: 734 5540

SOUTH AFRICA
W & A Textiles Ltd
60 Old Pretoria Road
Halfway House
Midrand 1685
Johannesburg
Tel: 011 805 0300

SPAIN
Usera Usera
Ayala 56, 28001 Madrid
Tel: 91 577 9461

SWEDEN
TAPI
Kommendörsgatan 22
114 48 Stockholm
Tel: 08 661 0380

SWITZERLAND
Ipso Facto SA
6 rue Joseph-Girard
1227 Geneva
Tel: 022 342 5077

TURKEY
A Day of Design
Atiye Sok 7/4
Ak Apt Tesvikiye 80200
Istanbul
Tel: 01 247 3206

UNITED ARAB EMIRATES
AATI
PO Box 2623
Dubai
Tel: 04 377 825

USA
Osborne & Little
65 Commerce Road
Stamford CT 06902
Tel: 203 359 1500

# DESIGNERS GUILD

is a registered trademark

Available from

# DESIGNERS GUILD STORE

267 Kings Road, London SW3 5EN

Tel: 071-351 5775

Upholstery,
painted and
contemporary
furniture,
fabric
accessories

Bedlinen,
blankets, rugs,
fragrances
and bathroom
accessories

Arts and Crafts —
ceramics, glass,
metalwork and
hand weaves

Country and
contemporary
tableware
including
'La Limonaia'
Italian
hand-painted
range

Tablelinen,
kitchen products
and speciality foods

# INDEX